MERCEDES-BENZ
SLK R170 series
1996-2004
Brian Long

Also from Veloce Publishing

Speedpro Series

- 4-Cylinder Engine Short Block High-Performance Manual – New Updated & Revised Edition (Hammill)
- Alfa Romeo DOHC High-performance Manual (Kartalamakis)
- Alfa Romeo V6 Engine High-performance Manual (Kartalamakis)
- BMC 998cc A-series Engine, How to Power Tune (Hammill)
- 1275cc A-series High-performance Manual (Hammill)
- Camshafts – How to Choose & Time Them For Maximum Power (Hammill)
- Competition Car Datalogging Manual, The (Templeman)
- Cylinder Heads, How to Build, Modify & Power Tune – Updated & Revised Edition (Burgess & Gollan)
- Distributor-type Ignition Systems, How to Build & Power Tune – New 3rd Edition (Hammill)
- Fast Road Car, How to Plan and Build – Revised & Updated Colour New Edition (Stapleton)
- Ford SOHC 'Pinto' & Sierra Cosworth DOHC Engines, How to Power Tune – Updated & Enlarged Edition (Hammill)
- Ford V8, How to Power Tune Small Block Engines (Hammill)
- Harley-Davidson Evolution Engines, How to Build & Power Tune (Hammill)
- Holley Carburetors, How to Build & Power Tune – Revised & Updated Edition (Hammill)
- Honda Civic Type R High-Performance Manual, The (Cowland & Clifford)
- Jaguar XK Engines, How to Power Tune – Revised & Updated Colour Edition (Hammill)
- Land Rover Discovery, Defender & Range Rover – How to Modify Coil Sprung Models for High Performance & Off-Road Action (Hosier)
- MG Midget & Austin-Healey Sprite, How to Power Tune – New 3rd Edition (Stapleton)
- MGB 4-cylinder Engine, How to Power Tune (Burgess)
- MGB V8 Power, How to Give Your – Third Colour Edition (Williams)
- MGB, MGC & MGB V8, How to Improve – New 2nd Edition (Williams)
- Mini Engines, How to Power Tune On a Small Budget – Colour Edition (Hammill)
- Motorcycle-engined Racing Car, How to Build (Pashley)
- Motorsport, Getting Started in (Collins)
- Nissan GT-R High-performance Manual, The (Gorodji)
- Nitrous Oxide High-performance Manual, The (Langfield)
- Race & Trackday Driving Techniques (Hornsey)
- Retro or classic car for high performance, How to modify your (Stapleton)
- Rover V8 Engines, How to Power Tune (Hammill)
- Secrets of Speed – Today's techniques for 4-stroke engine blueprinting & tuning (Swager)
- Sportscar & Kitcar Suspension & Brakes, How to Build & Modify – Revised 3rd Edition (Hammill)
- SU Carburettor High-performance Manual (Hammill)
- Successful Low-Cost Rally Car, How to Build a (Young)
- Suzuki 4x4, How to Modify For Serious Off-road Action (Richardson)
- Tiger Avon Sportscar, How to Build Your Own – Updated & Revised 2nd Edition (Dudley)
- TR2, 3 & TR4, How to Improve (Williams)
- TR5, 250 & TR6, How to Improve (Williams)
- TR7 & TR8, How to Improve (Williams)
- V8 Engine, How to Build a Short Block For High Performance (Hammill)
- Volkswagen Beetle Suspension, Brakes & Chassis, How to Modify For High Performance (Hale)
- Volkswagen Bus Suspension, Brakes & Chassis for High Performance, How to Modify – Updated & Enlarged New Edition (Hale)
- Weber DCOE, & Dellorto DHLA Carburetors, How to Build & Power Tune – 3rd Edition (Hammill)

RAC handbooks

- Caring for your car – How to maintain & service your car (Fry)
- Caring for your car's bodywork and interior (Nixon)
- Caring for your bicycle – How to maintain & repair your bicycle (Henshaw)
- How your motorcycle works – Your guide to the components & systems of modern motorcycles (Henshaw)
- Caring for your scooter – How to maintain & service your 49cc to 125cc twist & go scooter (Fry)
- Efficient Driver's Handbook, The (Moss)
- Electric Cars – The Future is Now! (Linde)
- First aid for your car – Your expert guide to common problems & how to fix them (Collins)
- How your car works (Linde)
- Motorcycles – A first-time-buyer's guide (Henshaw)
- Motorhomes – A first-time-buyer's guide (Fry)
- Pass the MoT test! – How to check & prepare your car for the annual MoT test (Paxton)
- Selling your car – How to make your car look great and how to sell it fast (Knight)
- Simple fixes for your car – How to do small jobs for yourself and save money (Collins)

Enthusiast's Restoration Manual Series

- Beginner's Guide to Classic Motorcycle Restoration YOUR step-by-step guide to setting up a workshop, choosing a project, dismantling, sourcing parts, renovating & rebuilding classic motorcyles from the 1970s & 1980s, The (Burns)
- Citroën 2CV, How to Restore (Porter)
- Classic Large Frame Vespa Scooters, How to Restore (Paxton)
- Classic Car Bodywork, How to Restore (Thaddeus)
- Classic British Car Electrical Systems (Astley)
- Classic Car Electrics (Thaddeus)
- Classic Cars, How to Paint (Thaddeus)
- Ducati Bevel Twins 1971 to 1986 (Falloon)
- How to restore Honda Fours – YOUR step-by-step colour illustrated guide to complete restoration (Burns)
- Jaguar E-type (Crespin)
- Reliant Regal, How to Restore (Payne)
- Triumph TR2, 3, 3A, 4 & 4A, How to Restore (Williams)
- Triumph TR5/250 & 6, How to Restore (Williams)
- Triumph TR7/8, How to Restore (Williams)
- Volkswagen Beetle, How to Restore (Tyler)
- VW Bay Window Bus (Paxton)
- Yamaha FS1-E, How to Restore (Watts)

Expert Guides

- Land Rover Series I-III – Your expert guide to common problems & how to fix them (Thurman)
- MG Midget & A-H Sprite – Your expert guide to common problems & how to fix them (Horler)

Essential Buyer's Guide Series

- Alfa Romeo Giulia GT Coupé (Booker)
- Alfa Romeo Giulia Spider (Booker)
- Audi TT (Davies)
- Austin Seven (Barker)
- Big Healeys (Trummel)
- BMW E21 3 Series (1975-1983) (Reverente)
- BMW E30 3 Series 1981 to 1994 (Hosier)
- BMW GS (Henshaw)
- BMW X5 (Saunders)
- BSA 350 & 500 Unit Construction Singles (Henshaw)
- BSA 500 & 650 Twins (Henshaw)
- BSA Bantam (Henshaw)
- Citroën 2CV (Paxton)
- Citroën ID & DS (Heilig)
- Cobra Replicas (Ayre)
- Corvette C2 Sting Ray 1963-1967 (Falconer)
- Ducati Bevel Twins (Falloon)
- Ducati Desmodue Twins (Falloon)
- Ducati Desmoquattro Twins - 851, 888, 916, 996, 998, ST4 1988 to 2004 (Falloon)
- Fiat 500 & 600 (Bobbitt)
- Ford Capri (Paxton)
- Ford Escort Mk1 & Mk2 (Williamson)
- Ford Mustang – First Generation 1964 to 1973 (Cook)
- Ford RS Cosworth Sierra & Escort (Williamson)
- Harley-Davidson Big Twins (Henshaw)
- Hinckley Triumph triples & fours 750, 900, 955, 1000, 1050, 1200 – 1991-2009 (Henshaw)
- Honda CBR FireBlade (Henshaw)
- Honda CBR600 Hurricane (Henshaw)
- Honda SOHC Fours 1969-1984 (Henshaw)
- Jaguar E-Type 3.8 & 4.2-litre (Crespin)
- Jaguar E-type V12 5.3-litre (Crespin)
- Jaguar Mark 1 & 2 (All models including Daimler 2.5-litre V8) 1955 to 1969 (Thorley)
- Jaguar S-Type – 1999 to 2007 (Thorley)
- Jaguar X-Type – 2001 to 2009 (Thorley)
- Jaguar XJ-S (Crespin)
- Jaguar XJ6, XJ8 & XJR (Thorley)
- Jaguar XK 120, 140 & 150 (Thorley)
- Jaguar XK8 & XKR (1996-2005) (Thorley)
- Jaguar/Daimler XJ 1994-2003 (Crespin)
- Jaguar/Daimler XJ40 (Crespin)
- Jaguar/Daimler XJ6, XJ12 & Sovereign (Crespin)
- Kawasaki Z1 & Z900 (Orritt)
- Land Rover Series I, II & IIA (Thurman)
- Land Rover Series III (Thurman)
- Lotus Seven replicas & Caterham 7: 1973-2013 (Hawkins)
- Mazda MX-5 Miata (Mk1 1989-97 & Mk2 98-2001) (Crook)
- Mercedes Benz Pagoda 230SL, 250SL & 280SL roadsters & coupès (Bass)
- Mercedes-Benz 280-560SL & SLC (Bass)
- MG Midget & A-H Sprite (Horler)
- MG TD, TF & TF1500 (Jones)
- MGA 1955-1962 (Crosier)
- MGB & MGB GT (Williams)
- MGF & MG TF (Hawkins)
- Mini (Paxton)
- Morris Minor & 1000 (Newell)
- Moto Guzzi 2-valve big twins (Falloon)
- New Mini (Collins)
- Norton Commando (Henshaw)
- Peugeot 205 GTI (Blackburn)
- Porsche 911 (964) (Streather)
- Porsche 911 (993) (Streather)
- Porsche 911 (996) (Streather)
- Porsche 911 Carrera 3.2 (Streather)
- Porsche 911SC (Streather)
- Porsche 924 – All models 1976 to 1988 (Hodgkins)
- Porsche 928 (Hemmings)
- Porsche 930 Turbo & 911 (930) Turbo (Streather)
- Porsche 944 (Higgins)
- Porsche 986 Boxster (Streather)
- Porsche 987 Boxster & Cayman (Streather)
- Rolls-Royce Silver Shadow & Bentley T-Series (Bobbitt)
- Subaru Impreza (Hobbs)
- Triumph 350 & 500 Twins (Henshaw)
- Triumph Bonneville (Henshaw)
- Triumph Herald & Vitesse (Davies)
- Triumph Spitfire & GT6 (Baugues)
- Triumph Stag (Mort)
- Triumph Thunderbird, Trophy & Tiger (Henshaw)
- Triumph TR6 (Williams)
- Triumph TR7 & TR8 (Williams)
- Vespa Scooters – Classic 2-stroke models 1960-2008 (Paxton)
- Volvo 700/900 Series (Beavis)
- VW Beetle (Cservenka & Copping)
- VW Bus (Cservenka & Copping)
- VW Golf GTI (Cservenka & Copping)

Those Were The Days ... Series

- Alpine Trials & Rallies 1910-1973 (Pfundner)
- American 'Independent' Automakers – AMC to Willys 1945 to 1960 (Mort)
- American Station Wagons – The Golden Era 1950-1975 (Mort)
- American Trucks of the 1950s (Mort)
- American Trucks of the 1960s (Mort)
- American Woodies 1928-1953 (Mort)
- Anglo-American Cars from the 1930s to the 1970s (Mort)
- Austerity Motoring (Bobbitt)
- Austins, The last real (Peck)
- Brighton National Speed Trials (Gardiner)
- British and European Trucks of the 1970s (Peck)
- British Drag Racing – The early years (Pettitt)
- British Lorries of the 1950s (Bobbitt)
- British Lorries of the 1960s (Bobbitt)
- British Touring Car Racing (Collins)
- British Police Cars (Walker)
- British Woodies (Peck)
- Café Racer Phenomenon, The (Walker)
- Don Hayter's MGB Story – - The birth of the MGB in MG's Abingdon Design & Development Office (Hayter)
- Drag Bike Racing in Britain – From the mid '60s to the mid '80s (Lee)
- Dune Buggy Phenomenon, The (Hale)
- Dune Buggy Phenomenon Volume 2, The (Hale)
- Endurance Racing at Silverstone in the 1970s & 1980s (Parker)
- Hot Rod & Stock Car Racing in Britain in the 1980s (Neil)
- Last Real Austins 1946-1959, The (Peck)
- MG's Abingdon Factory (Moylan)
- Motor Racing at Brands Hatch in the Seventies (Parker)
- Motor Racing at Brands Hatch in the Eighties (Parker)
- Motor Racing at Crystal Palace (Collins)
- Motor Racing at Goodwood in the Sixties (Gardiner)
- Motor Racing at Nassau in the 1950s & 1960s (O'Neil)
- Motor Racing at Oulton Park in the 1960s (McFadyen)
- Motor Racing at Oulton Park in the 1970s (McFadyen)
- Motor Racing at Thruxton in the 1970s (Grant-Braham)
- Motor Racing at Thruxton in the 1980s (Grant-Braham)
- Superprix – The Story of Birmingham Motor Race (Page & Collins)
- Three Wheelers (Bobbitt)

Truckmakers

- DAF Trucks since 1949 (Peck)
- Mercedes-Benz Trucks (Peck)

Auto-Graphics Series

- Fiat-based Abarths (Sparrow)
- Jaguar MKI & II Saloons (Sparrow)
- Lambretta Li Series Scooters (Sparrow)

Rally Giants Series

- Audi Quattro (Robson)
- Austin Healey 100-6 & 3000 (Robson)
- Fiat 131 Abarth (Robson)
- Ford Escort MkI (Robson)
- Ford Escort RS Cosworth & World Rally Car (Robson)
- Ford Escort RS1800 (Robson)
- Lancia Delta 4WD/Integrale (Robson)
- Lancia Stratos (Robson)
- Mini Cooper/Mini Cooper S (Robson)
- Peugeot 205 T16 (Robson)
- Saab 96 & V4 (Robson)
- Subaru Impreza (Robson)
- Toyota Celica GT4 (Robson)

WSC Giants

- Audi R8 (Wagstaff)
- Ferrari 312P & 312PB (Collins & McDonough)
- Gulf-Mirage 1967 to 1982 (McDonough)
- Matra Sports Cars – MS620, 630, 650, 660 & 670 – 1966 to 1974 (McDonough)

Biographies

- A Chequered Life – Graham Warner and the Chequered Flag (Hesletine)
- Amédée Gordini ... a true racing legend (Smith)
- André Lefebvre, and the cars he created at Voisin and Citroën (Beck)
- Cliff Allison, The Official Biography of – From the Fells to Ferrari (Gauld)
- Edward Turner – The Man Behind the Motorcycles (Clew)
- Driven by Desire – The Desiré Wilson Story
- First Principles – The Official Biography of Keith Duckworth (Burr)
- Inspired to Design – F1 cars, Indycars & racing tyres: the autobiography of Nigel Bennett (Bennett)
- Jack Sears, The Official Biography of – Gentleman Jack (Gauld)
- Jim Redman – 6 Times World Motorcycle Champion: The Autobiography (Redman)
- John Chatham – 'Mr Big Healey' – The Official Biography (Burr)
- The Lee Noble Story (Wilkins)
- Mason's Motoring Mayhem – Tony Mason's hectic life in motorsport and television (Mason)
- Pat Moss Carlsson Story, The – Harnessing Horsepower (Turner)
- Tony Robinson – The biography of a race mechanic (Wagstaff)
- Virgil Exner – Visioneer: The Official Biography of Virgil M Exner Designer Extraordinaire (Grist)

Toys & models

- Britains Farm Model Balers & Combines 1967-2007, Pocket Guide to (Pullen)
- Britains Farm Model & Toy Tractors 1998-2008, Pocket Guide to (Pullen)
- Britains Toy Models Catalogues 1970-1979 (Pullen)
- British Toy Boats 1920 onwards – A pictorial tribute (Gillham)
- Diecast Toy Cars of the 1950s & 1960s (Ralston)
- Ford In Miniature (Olson)
- GM In Miniature (Olson)
- Plastic Toy Cars of the 1950s & 1960s (Ralston)
- Tinplate Toy Cars of the 1950s & 1960s (Ralston)

General

- 11/2-litre GP Racing 1961-1965 (Whitelock)
- AC Two-litre Saloons & Buckland Sportscars (Archibald)
- Alfa Romeo 155/156/147 Competition Touring Cars (Collins)
- Alfa Romeo Giulia Coupé GT & GTA (Tipler)
- Alfa Romeo Montreal – The dream car that came true (Taylor)
- Alfa Romeo Montreal – The Essential Companion (Taylor)
- Alfa Tipo 33 (McDonough & Collins)
- Alpine & Renault – The Development of the Revolutionary Turbo F1 Car 1968 to 1979 (Smith)
- Alpine & Renault – The Sports Prototypes 1963 to 1969 (Smith)
- Alpine & Renault – The Sports Prototypes 1973 to 1978 (Smith)
- Anatomy of the Works Minis (Moylan)
- Armstrong-Siddeley (Smith)
- Art Deco and British Car Design (Down)
- Autodrome (Collins & Ireland)
- Autodrome 2 (Collins & Ireland)
- Automotive A-Z, Lane's Dictionary of Automotive Terms (Lane)
- Automotive Mascots (Kay & Springate)
- Bahamas Speed Weeks, The (O'Neil)
- Bentley Continental, Corniche and Azure (Bennett)
- Bentley MkVI, Rolls-Royce Silver Wraith, Dawn & Cloud/Bentley R & S-Series (Nutland)
- Bluebird CN7 (Stevens)
- BMC Competitions Department Secrets (Turner, Chambers & Browning)
- BMW 5-Series (Cranswick)
- BMW Z-Cars (Taylor)
- BMW Boxer Twins 1970-1995 Bible, The (Falloon)
- BMW Cafe Racers (Cloesen)
- BMW Custom Motorcycles – Choppers, Cruisers, Bobbers, Trikes & Quads (Cloesen)
- BMW – The Power of M (Vivian)
- Bonjour – Is this Italy? (Turner)
- British 250cc Racing Motorcycles (Pereira)
- British at Indianapolis, The (Wagstaff)
- British Cars, The Complete Catalogue of, 1895-1975 (Culshaw & Horrobin)
- BRM – A Mechanic's Tale (Salmon)
- BRM V16 (Ludvigsen)
- BSA Bantam Bible, The (Henshaw)
- BSA Motorcycles - the final evolution (Jones)
- Bugatti Type 40 (Price)
- Bugatti 46/50 Updated Edition (Price & Arbey)
- Bugatti T44 & T49 (Price & Arbey)
- Bugatti 57 2nd Edition (Price)
- Caravan, Improve & Modify Your (Porter)
- Caravans, The Illustrated History 1919-1959 (Jenkinson)
- Caravans, The Illustrated History From 1960 (Jenkinson)
- Carrera Panamericana, La (Tipler)
- Chrysler 300 – America's Most Powerful Car 2nd Edition (Ackerson)
- Chrysler PT Cruiser (Ackerson)
- Citroën DS (Bobbitt)
- Classic British Car Electrical Systems (Astley)
- Cobra – The Real Thing! (Legate)
- Concept Cars, How to illustrate and design (Dewey)
- Cortina – Ford's Bestseller (Robson)
- Coventry Climax Racing Engines (Hammill)
- Daily Mirror 1970 World Cup Rally 40, The (Robson)
- Daimler SP250 New Edition (Long)
- Datsun Fairlady Roadster to 280ZX – The Z-Car Story (Long)
- Dino – The V6 Ferrari (Long)
- Dodge Challenger & Plymouth Barracuda (Grist)
- Dodge Charger – Enduring Thunder (Ackerson)
- Dodge Dynamite! (Grist)
- Draw & Paint Cars – How to (Gardiner)
- Drive on the Wild Side, A – 20 Extreme Driving Adventures From Around the World (Weaver)
- Ducati 750 Bible, The (Falloon)
- Ducati 750 SS 'round-case' 1974, The Book of the (Falloon)
- Ducati 860, 900 and Mille Bible, The (Falloon)
- Ducati Monster Bible, The (Falloon)
- Dune Buggy, Building A – The Essential Manual (Shakespeare)
- Dune Buggy Files (Hale)
- Dune Buggy Handbook (Hale)
- East German Motor Vehicles in Pictures (Suhr/Weinreich)
- Fast Ladies – Female Racing Drivers 1888 to 1970 (Bouzanquet)
- Fate of the Sleeping Beauties, The (op de Weegh/Hottendorff/op de Weegh)
- Ferrari 288 GTO, The Book of the (Sackey)
- Fiat & Abarth 124 Spider & Coupé (Tipler)
- Fiat & Abarth 500 & 600 – 2nd Edition (Bobbitt)
- Fiats, Great Small (Ward)
- Fine Art of the Motorcycle Engine, The (Peirce)
- Ford Cleveland 335-Series V8 engine 1970 to 1982 – The Essential Source Book (Hammill)
- Ford F100/F150 Pick-up 1948-1996 (Ackerson)
- Ford F150 Pick-up 1997-2005 (Ackerson)
- Ford GT – Then, and Now (Streather)
- Ford GT40 (Legate)
- Ford Model Y (Roberts)
- Ford Thunderbird From 1954, The Book of the (Long)
- Formula 5000 Motor Racing, Back then ... and back now (Lawson)
- Forza Minardi! (Vigar)
- France: the essential guide for car enthusiasts – 200 things for the car enthusiast to see and do (Parish)
- From Crystal Palace to Red Square – - A Hapless Biker's Road to Russia (Turner)
- Funky Mopeds (Skelton)
- Grand Prix Ferrari – The Years of Enzo Ferrari's Power, 1948-1980 (Pritchard)
- Grand Prix Ford – DFV-powered Formula 1 Cars (Pritchard)
- GT – The World's Best GT Cars 1953-73 (Dawson)
- Hillclimbing & Sprinting – The Essential Manual (Short & Wilkinson)
- Honda NSX (Long)
- Intermeccanica – The Story of the Prancing Bull (McCredie & Reisner)
- Italian Cafe Racers (Cloesen)
- Italian Custom Motorcycles (Cloesen)
- Jaguar, The Rise of (Price)
- Jaguar XJ 220 – The Inside Story (Moreton)
- Jaguar XJ-S, The Book of the (Long)
- Jeep CJ (Ackerson)
- Jeep Wrangler (Ackerson)
- Karmann-Ghia Coupé & Convertible (Bobbitt)
- Kawasaki Triples Bible, The (Walker)
- Kris Meeke – Intercontinental Rally Challenge Champion (McBride)
- Lamborghini Miura Bible, The (Sackey)
- Lamborghini Urraco, The Book of the (Landsem)
- Lambretta Bible, The (Davies)
- Lancia 037 (Collins)
- Lancia Delta HF Integrale (Blaettel & Wagner)
- Land Rover Series III Reborn (Porter)
- Land Rover, The Half-ton Military (Cook)
- Laverda Twins & Triples Bible 1968-1986 (Falloon)
- Lea-Francis Story, The (Price)
- Le Mans Panoramic (Ireland)
- Lexus Story, The (Long)
- Little book of microcars, the (Quellin)
- Little book of smart, the – New Edition (Jackson)
- Little book of trikes, the (Quellin)
- Lola – The Illustrated History (1957-1977) (Starkey)
- Lola – All the Sports Racing & Single-seater Racing Cars 1978-1997 (Starkey)
- Lola T70 – The Racing History & Individual Chassis Record – 4th Edition (Starkey)
- Lotus 49 (Oliver)
- Marketingmobiles, The Wonderful Wacky World of (Hale)
- Maserati 250F In Focus (Pritchard)
- Mazda MX-5/Miata 1.6 Enthusiast's Workshop Manual (Grainger & Shoemark)
- Mazda MX-5/Miata 1.8 Enthusiast's Workshop Manual (Grainger & Shoemark)
- Mazda MX-5 Miata: The Book of the World's Favourite Sportscar (Long)
- Mazda MX-5 Miata Roadster (Long)
- Maximum Mini (Booij)
- Meet the English (Bowie)
- Mercedes-Benz SL – W113-series 1963-1971 (Long)
- Mercedes-Benz SL & SLC – 107-series 1971-1989 (Long)
- Mercedes-Benz SLK – R170 series 1996-2004 (Long)
- MGA (Price Williams)
- MGB & MGB GT– Expert Guide (Auto-doc Series) (Williams)
- MGB Electrical Systems Updated & Revised Edition (Astley)
- Micro Caravans (Jenkinson)
- Micro Trucks (Mort)
- Microcars at Large! (Quellin)
- Mini Cooper – The Real Thing! (Tipler)
- Mini Minor to Asia Minor (West)
- Mitsubishi Lancer Evo, The Road Car & WRC Story (Long)
- Montlhéry, The Story of the Paris Autodrome (Boddy)
- Morgan Maverick (Lawrence)
- Morris Minor, 60 Years on the Road (Newell)
- Moto Guzzi Sport & Le Mans Bible, The (Falloon)
- Motor Movies – The Posters! (Veysey)
- Motor Racing – Reflections of a Lost Era (Carter)
- Motor Racing – The Pursuit of Victory 1930-1962 (Carter)
- Motor Racing – The Pursuit of Victory 1963-1972 (Wyatt/Sears)
- Motor Racing Heroes – The Stories of 100 Greats (Newman)
- Motorcycle Apprentice (Cakebread)
- Motorcycle GP Racing in the 1960s (Pereira)
- Motorcycle Road & Racing Chassis Designs (Noakes)
- Motorhomes, The Illustrated History (Jenkinson)
- Motorsport In colour, 1950s (Wainwright)
- MV Agusta Fours, The book of the classic (Falloon)
- Nissan 300ZX & 350Z – The Z-Car Story (Long)
- Nissan GT-R Supercar: Born to race (Gorodji)
- Northeast American Sports Car Races 1950-1959 (O'Neil)
- Nothing Runs – Misadventures in the Classic, Collectable & Exotic Car Biz (Slutsky)
- Off-Road Giants! (Volume 1) – Heroes of 1960s Motorcycle Sport (Westlake)
- Off-Road Giants! (Volume 2) – Heroes of 1960s Motorcycle Sport (Westlake)
- Pass the Theory and Practical Driving Tests (Gibson & Hoole)
- Peking to Paris 2007 (Young)
- Pontiac Firebird (Cranswick)
- Porsche Boxster (Long)
- Porsche 356 (2nd Edition) (Long)
- Porsche 908 (Födisch, Neßhöver, Roßbach, Schwarz & Roßbach)
- Porsche 911 Carrera – The Last of the Evolution (Corlett)
- Porsche 911R, RS & RSR, 4th Edition (Starkey)
- Porsche 911, The Book of the (Long)
- Porsche 911SC 'Super Carrera' – The Essential Companion (Streather)
- Porsche 914 & 914-6: The Definitive History of the Road & Competition Cars (Long)
- Porsche 924 (Long)
- The Porsche 924 Carreras - evolution to excellence (Smith)
- Porsche 928 (Long)
- Porsche 944 (Long)
- Porsche 964, 993 & 996 Data Plate Code Breaker (Streather)
- Porsche 993 'King Of Porsche' – The Essential Companion (Streather)
- Porsche 996 'Supreme Porsche' – The Essential Companion (Streather)
- Porsche Racing Cars – 1953 to 1975 (Long)
- Porsche Racing Cars – 1976 to 2005 (Long)
- Porsche – The Rally Story (Meredith)
- Porsche: Three Generations of Genius (Meredith)
- Preston Tucker & Others (Linde)
- RAC Rally Action! (Gardiner)
- RACING COLOURS – MOTOR RACING COMPOSITIONS 1908-2009 (Newman)
- Rallye Sport Fords: The Inside Story (Moreton)
- Roads with a View – England's greatest views and how to find them by road (Corfield)
- Roads With a View – Wales' greatest views and how to find them by road (Corfield)
- Rolls-Royce Silver Shadow/Bentley T Series Corniche & Camargue – Revised & Enlarged Edition (Bobbitt)
- Rolls-Royce Silver Spirit, Silver Spur & Bentley Mulsanne 2nd Edition (Bobbitt)
- Runways & Racers (O'Neil)
- Russian Motor Vehicles – Soviet Limousines 1930-2003 (Kelly)
- Russian Motor Vehicles – The Czarist Period 1784 to 1917 (Kelly)
- RX-7 – Mazda's Rotary Engine Sportscar (Updated & Revised New Edition) (Long)
- Scooters & Microcars, The A-Z of Popular (Dan)
- Scooter Lifestyle (Grainger)
- SCOOTER MANIA! – - Recollections of the Isle of Man International Scooter Rally (Jackson)
- Singer Story: Cars, Commercial Vehicles, Bicycles & Motorcycle (Atkinson)
- Sleeping Beauties USA – abandoned classic cars & trucks (Marek)
- SM – Citroën's Maserati-engined Supercar (Long & Claverol)
- Speedway – Auto racing's ghost tracks (Collins & Ireland)
- Sprite Caravans, The Story of (Jenkinson)
- Standard Motor Company, The Book of the
- Subaru Impreza: The Road Car And WRC Story (Long)
- Supercar, How to Build your own (Thompson)
- Tales from the Toolbox (Oliver)
- Taxi! The Story of the 'London' Taxicab (Bobbitt)
- Toleman Story, The (Hilton)
- Toyota Celica & Supra, The Book of Toyota's Sports Coupés (Long)
- Toyota MR2 Coupés & Spyders (Long)
- Triumph Bonneville Bible (59-83) (Henshaw)
- Triumph Bonneville!, Save the – The inside story of the Meriden Workers' Co-op (Rosamond)
- Triumph Motorcycles & the Meriden Factory (Hancox)
- Triumph Speed Twin & Thunderbird Bible (Woolridge)
- Triumph Tiger Cub Bible (Estall)
- Triumph Trophy Bible (Woolridge)
- Triumph TR6 (Kimberley)
- TT Talking - The TT's most exciting era – As seen by Manx Radio TT's lead commentator 2004-2012 (Lambert)
- TWR Story, The – Group A (Hughes & Scott)
- Unraced (Collins)
- Velocette Motorcycles – MSS to Thruxton – New Third Edition (Burris)
- Volkswagen Bus Book, The (Bobbitt)
- Volkswagen Bus or Van to Camper, How to Convert (Porter)
- Volkswagens of the World (Glen)
- VW Beetle Cabriolet – The full story of the convertible Beetle (Bobbitt)
- VW Beetle – The Car of the 20th Century (Copping)
- VW Bus – 40 Years of Splitties, Bays & Wedges (Copping)
- VW Bus Book, The (Bobbitt)
- VW Golf: Five Generations of Fun (Copping & Cservenka)
- VW – The Air-cooled Era (Copping)
- VW T5 Camper Conversion Manual (Porter)
- VW Campers (Copping)
- Which Oil? – Choosing the right oils & greases for your antique, vintage, veteran, classic or collector car (Michell)
- Works Minis, The Last (Purves & Brenchley)
- Works Rally Mechanic (Moylan)

From Veloce Publishing's other imprints:

Battle Cry!

- Soviet General & field rank officer uniforms: 1955 to 1991 (Streather)
- Red & Soviet military & paramilitary services: female uniforms 1941-1991 (Streather)

Hubble & Hattie

- A dog's dinner – Practical, healthy and nutritious recipes for REAL dog food (Paton-Ayre)
- Animal Grief – How animals mourn (Alderton)
- Camper vans, ex-pats and Spanish hounds – The strays of Spain: from road trip to rescue (Coates)
- Cat Speak – recognising and understanding behaviour (Rauth-Widmann)
- Clever Dog! – life lessons from the world's most successful animal (O'Meara)
- Dieting with my dog – One busy life, two full figures ... and unconditional love (Frezon)
- Dinner with Rover – Delicious, nutritious meals for you and your dog to share (Paton-Ayre)
- Dog Cookies – Healthy allergen-free treat recipes for your dog (Schops, Pick)
- Dog Games – Stimulating play to entertain your dog and you (Blenski)
- Dog Relax – Relaxed dogs, relaxed owners (Pilguj)
- Dog Speak – recognising and understanding behaviour (Blenski)
- Dog-friendly Gardening – Creating a safe haven for you and your dog (Bush)
- Dogs on wheels – Travelling with your canine companion (Mort)
- Emergency first aid for dogs – at home and away (Bucksch)
- Exercising your puppy: a gentle & natural approach – Gentle Dog care (Robertson, Pope)
- Fun and games for cats! (Seidl)
- Helping minds meet – Skills for a better life with your dog (Zulch, Mills, Baumber)
- Know Your Dog – The guide to a beautiful relationship (Birmelin)
- Life skills for puppies – Laying the foundation for a loving, lasting relationship (Zulch, Mills, Baumber)
- Life skills for puppies – Laying the foundation for a loving, lasting relationship (Millsm, Zulch, Baumber)
- Living with an Older Dog – Gentle Dog Care (Alderton, Hall)
- Miaow! Cats really are nicer than people! (Moore CBE FRS)
- My cat has arthritis ... but lives life to the full! (Carrick)
- My dog has arthritis ... but lives life to the full! (Carrick)
- My dog has cruciate ligament injury – but lives life to the full! A practical guide for owners (Häusler, Friedrich)
- My dog has epilepsy ... but lives life to the full! (Carrick)
- My dog has hip dysplasia ... but lives life to the full! (Häusle, Friedrich)
- My dog is blind – but lives life to the full! The guide to every aspect of a happy life with a blind or sight-impaired dog (Horsky)
- My dog is deaf – but lives life to the full! (Willms)
- My Dog, my Friend. Heart-warming tales of canine companionship from celebrities and other extraordinary people (Gordon)
- No walks? No worries! Maintaining wellbeing in dogs on restricted exercise (Ryan, Zulch, Baumber)
- Partners – Everyday working dogs being heroes every day (Walton)
- Smellorama! Nose games for dogs (Theby)
- Swim to recovery: canine hydrotherapy healing – Gentle Dog Care (Wong)
- The Complete Dog Massage Manual – Gentle Dog Care (Robertson)
- The Rex Factor – my dog, my friend (Gordon)
- The truth about wolves and dogs – Dispelling the myths of dog training (Shelbourne)
- Waggy Tails & Wheelchairs – The complete guide to harmonious living for you and your dog (Epp)
- Walking the dog – Motorway walks for drivers and dogs (Rees)
- Winston ... the dog who changed my life (Klute)
- You and Your Border Terrier – The Essential Guide (Alderton)
- You and Your Cockapoo – The Essential Guide (Alderton)

First published November 2014. Reprinted January 2015 by Veloce Publishing Limited, Veloce House, Parkway Farm Business Park, Middle Farm Way, Poundbury, Dorchester, Dorset, DT1 3AR, England. Fax 01305 250479/email info@veloce.co.uk/web www.veloce.co.uk or www.velocebooks.com.

ISBN: 978-1-845846-51-0 UPC: 6-36847-04651-4 Readers with ideas for automotive books, or books on other transport or related hobby subjects, are invited to write to the editorial director of Veloce Publishing at the above address. British Library Cataloguing in Publication Data – A catalogue record for this book is available from the British Library. Typesetting, design and page make-up all by Veloce Publishing Ltd on Apple Mac. Printed in India by Imprint Press.

For post publication news, updates and amendments relating to this book please visit: www.veloce.co.uk/books/V4651

www.veloce.co.uk

MERCEDES-BENZ
SLK R170 series

1996-2004

Brian Long

Contents

Introduction

Over the years, the SL sports car – the jewel in the Mercedes-Benz crown – grew bigger and bigger, with its sticker price rising at a similar rate to its weight. Indeed, by the time the V12 version came along, one could almost buy a Rolls-Royce for similar money. The good people in Stuttgart realized this, and, prompted by the success of the Mazda MX-5 Miata, set about producing a smaller two-seater that was not only more affordable, but still had all the qualities one expects of a car carrying the three-pointed star on its nose. The end result was the R170 SLK, officially launched in 1996, and duly face-lifted in the year 2000. This book traces its history, from initial development through to the last one built in the spring of 2004, taking in all the variations in each of the main markets in-between …

Acknowledgements

As always, because of the use of contemporary photography as a matter of policy, these books cannot possibly be done without a great deal of help from the factory. As with my earlier SL books, I would particularly like to record my sincere appreciation for the services of Gerhard Heidbrink at Daimler AG in Stuttgart – a more helpful chap would be hard to find, and this book simply wouldn't have been possible without his kind co-operation.

I should also like to thank Nils Beckmann and Joerg Rupp in Stuttgart for managing to drag me into the 21st century on the parts book front, Kenichi Kobayashi at Miki Press, the extensive research facilities at the Japan Motor Industry Federation (JMIF) in Tokyo, Rob Halloway at Mercedes-Benz UK, and Robert Moran and Christian Bokich of Mercedes-Benz USA. There have been many, many others, but to list them all would take another book!

For past owners, present owners, those thinking of ownership, or simply followers of Mercedes-Benz lore, I really hope that you will enjoy this book, which will soon have a sister title on the R171 to go with it, also published by Veloce.

Brian Long
Chiba City, Japan

S LK 9608

SLK 320
S MJ 1844

1

HISTORY OF THE BRAND

The name Mercedes-Benz, along with the three-pointed star trademark that goes with it, is recognised the world over as a symbol of prestige, exemplifying the highest levels of German engineering and quality. Before moving on to the book's main subject, it's worthwhile reflecting on the history of the brand, and what made it so renowned, to help put things into perspective …

The Mercedes-Benz story begins with two pioneers of the motor industry: Gottlieb Daimler, and Carl Benz. Somewhat surprisingly, despite the fact that both were German-born, with both of them recognised as leading lights in the fledgling automotive trade, based less than 60 miles (100km) away from each other, they never actually met. Nonetheless, the coming together of the two companies they founded is what concerns us here, with the Daimler-Benz business using the Mercedes-Benz badge on the majority of its road vehicles from the late-1920s onwards.

Gottlieb Daimler (1834-1900).

Birth of the Daimler marque

Gottlieb Daimler was born in Schorndorf, a stone's throw to the east of Stuttgart, on 17 March 1834. Daimler didn't come from an engineering background (in fact, his father was a baker), but it was obvious from an early age that this was to be his destiny, for as well as learning Latin, he attended technical drawing school as a young boy.

Although he started his apprenticeship with a local gunsmith, as soon as his four years were up he began studying engineering in greater depth, augmenting his academic work with practical experience gained in the field in France and Britain.

On settling back in Germany, Daimler moved around for a while, although his appointment as Technical Director of the Gasmotoren-Fabrik Deutz AG (founded by Nikolaus August Otto

The first Daimler car, built in 1886, featured on a German postage stamp released 75 years later in 1961.

– the father of the four-stroke, 'Otto-cycle' engine) in 1872 was an important step in his career, with Wilhelm Maybach (1846-1929), whom he'd first met as a colleague in 1864, already present as his right-hand man.

However, a rift between Daimler and the Cologne-based manufacturer grew in time, with Daimler and Maybach wanting to develop faster-running petrol engines that could release more power. Ultimately, in 1882, Gottlieb Daimler decided to go it alone and opened a small workshop at the back of his villa in Cannstatt, on the outskirts of Stuttgart, with Maybach working alongside him to help nurture this new technology.

A number of single-cylinder, air-cooled petrol engines were duly designed and built, one being used to power the world's first motorcycle in 1885. There was also a four-wheeled horseless carriage, actually produced for Daimler's wife as a birthday present, which made its initial runs during the autumn of 1886. Within a short space of time, the engines were finding various applications on land, rail, water, and even in the air. After building a second car in 1889, this time powered by a water-cooled V-twin, it was obvious that Daimler and Maybach were moving in the right direction, and investors soon started knocking on the door of the large new factory in Cannstatt.

The Daimler Motoren Gesellschaft (DMG) was registered on 28 November 1890, its purpose being to manufacture and market Daimler engines and related products. In addition, there was a great deal of licensing activity in this new and exciting field of engineering, with Panhard & Levassor of France being one of the first to sign up. There was also a company founded in America bearing Daimler's name (with William Steinway of Steinway piano fame behind it), and another in England thanks to the business dealings of Frederick Simms and Harry Lawson.

As so often happens once investors get involved, though, profits start to dominate decisions, and the desire to experiment usually has to be tempered with the sale of products to satisfy short-term requirements. Maybach was forced to leave the Cannstatt company due to a clash of policy, and Daimler's health was failing – a situation not helped by the internal conflict with members of the DMG Board. Perhaps not surprisingly, Daimler ultimately resigned from the company he'd founded in October 1894.

Daimler and Maybach duly joined forces again (they'd remained close friends even after the latter left the DMG), this time bringing Daimler's son, Paul, into the fold. Between them they designed a 2.1-litre four-cylinder engine equipped with Maybach's innovative spray-nozzle carburettor. Known as the Phönix, it was a landmark unit, and, following some political manoeuvring from Frederick Simms, the pair was asked to return to the Daimler Motoren Gesellschaft on new, more favourable terms.

Gottlieb Daimler died on 6 March 1900, although Wilhelm Maybach continued his work before becoming heavily involved with aero-engine production for the famous Zeppelin airship concern. After the Great War, Maybach marketed a short-lived series of luxury cars under his own name, with the brand being revived recently for a Mercedes-Benz flagship saloon.

Genesis of the Benz brand

Carl Benz was born in Mühlberg on 25 November 1844. The son of a train driver, after leaving school he went to the Karlsruhe Polytechnic to study mechanical engineering. Following his graduation, he duly moved around a number of firms, gaining

Carl Benz (1844-1929).

Carl Benz and his family pictured with a Benz Viktoria of 1893 vintage.

practical experience in a wide range of fields, from building locomotives, to designing machinery and even iron bridges.

Joining forces with August Ritter, Benz established his own engineering shop in Mannheim, about 55 miles (90km) north of Stuttgart, in August 1871, but the partnership was short-lived, with Benz ultimately buying Ritter out. The small workshop was not a success, though, and Benz turned his attention to developing two-stroke engines (there were too many patents already registered against four-stroke powerplants) in the second half of 1877, with the first unit running successfully two years later.

By late-1882, the Benz engine had attracted investors, and Gasmotorenfabrik Mannheim was established, although Benz left the company within a few months of starting it as the shareholders tried to influence things too much. For instance, Benz wanted to produce a motor vehicle, but a quick financial return on supplying engines was favoured by the majority of people. Having put up production facilities as his stake in the business, Carl Benz was left no option but to start again from scratch.

Luckily, on 1 October 1883, Max Rose and Friedrich Esslinger came to Benz's aid in helping to form a new company, Benz & Co Rheinische Gasmotorenfabrik, Mannheim. Not long after, many of the patents applying to the four-stroke engine were declared null and void, allowing Benz to start developing a new, fast-running powerplant based on the Otto-cycle. By 29 January 1886, a patent had been filed on the world's first purpose-built vehicle to be powered by a petrol engine – the three-wheeled Benz Patent Motorwagon. Refinements were made, and the car was duly put into series production, the 'Model 3' version thereby providing the foundation stone for the automotive industry.

Ironically, in the spring of 1890, despite Benz & Co being Germany's second largest engine manufacturer, Carl Benz once again found himself alone in business. New partners were promptly found, and Benz continued to innovate, with four-wheeled cars being produced, new steering systems designed,

A 12/16hp Mercédès from 1901 – a more civilized version of the 35hp model that gave birth to the Mercédès brand.

The Daimler Motoren Gesellschaft (DMG) works at Untertürkheim, pictured in 1904.

and the horizontally-opposed (boxer) engine being developed, amongst other things.

The four-wheeled Velo, introduced in April 1894, was a huge commercial success by the standards of the day (around 1200 were built), allowing a new company, Benz & Cie AG, to be registered in May 1899. However, blinded by their bid to try and compete with a flood of cheaper machines built in France, Benz had become disillusioned with the people running the firm and resigned in January 1903.

A new century, a new age

Daimler and Benz were still rivals at the turn of the century, the companies bearing their names fighting in the showrooms graced by the rich and famous, and in the long-distance races and hillclimbs of Europe.

As it happens, the competition link provided the birth of the Mercedes brand. Shortly after Gottlieb Daimler passed away, Emil Jellinek (an Austrian businessman who, among other things, sold Daimlers to wealthy clients in the south of France) entered a couple of Daimlers in the Nice-La Turbie hillclimb using his pseudonym 'Mercédès' – the name of his daughter.

Following the fatal accident of one of the drivers, Jellinek proposed a number of changes that would not only improve safety, but also enhance the sporting nature of the vehicles to satisfy the needs of his customers. He requested a reduction in weight, a lower body, and a longer wheelbase in order to cope with the greater power outputs he outlined. Jellinek promised to purchase a large number of these vehicles in return for distribution rights in France, Belgium, the Austro-Hungarian Empire and America, but also requested that they carry the Mercédès badge.

A deal was struck on 2 April 1900, and Wilhelm Maybach set about designing the first Mercédès in conjunction with Paul Daimler without delay. By the end of the year, Jellinek had taken delivery of the first of the line – a racing car that ultimately provided the foundation stone for the modern automobile, with a low-slung, pressed steel chassis frame playing host to a 5.9-litre, 35hp engine cooled by a honeycomb radiator, and a gate for the gearchange.

A 1904 28/32hp Mercédès-Simplex. By this time, Daimler in Coventry, England, had long since found its own direction in terms of design and manufacturing, but William Steinway of piano fame would soon begin building Mercédès cars under licence in the States.

A Mercédès-Knight 16/45hp racer, powered by a Knight sleeve-valve engine, and pictured in Belgium in 1913. Both the Mercédès and Benz marques were highly-successful in top class competition at this time, not only in Europe, but America, too.

Mercédès advertising from 1922.

The Mercédès was raced with a great deal of success, and many variations were produced for regular road use, from an 8/11hp version all the way up to a 9.2-litre 60hp model. The Mercédès (the name being registered as a trademark by the DMG in 1902), set the standard for the day in the high-class car market, and was built under licence by numerous manufacturers.

Luckily, the DMG Board had made preparations for expansion in advance of its commercial success, buying a large piece of land in Untertürkheim, on the eastern edge of Stuttgart, in August 1900. This would duly become the spiritual home of Mercedes-Benz, becoming operational at the end of 1903.

Six-cylinder engines followed in 1906, and there was a limited run of Knight sleeve-valve models just before the First World War. Meanwhile, the famous three-pointed star had been registered as a trademark, with approval eventually coming in February 1911. The three arms within the three-pointed star represent the land, sea and air, and indeed each has been conquered in the Stuttgart company's own inimitable way over the years; the outer ring was first added in 1921.

Shortly after the Great War, when the conflict had, if nothing else, allowed technology, metallurgy and production techniques to make great advances, the first supercharged Mercédès made its debut, and on 30 April 1923, Ferdinand Porsche was drafted in from Austro-Daimler to replace Paul Daimler as Chief Engineer, bringing overhead camshafts and front-wheel brakes to the marque in a series of exceptionally elegant supercharged models.

In the meantime, Benz & Cie AG came to the fore, modernising its range via conventional two- and four-cylinder cars designed by Marius Barbarou. The move towards reasonably-priced machines allowed the Benz business to clock up world-leading sales of around 600 units a year at the turn of the century, but the policy was out of step with that of Carl Benz himself. As mentioned earlier, he gave up his post as Chief Engineer, although he did remain on the Supervisory Board until his death on 4 April 1929.

While all this political manoeuvring was going on, Carl Benz had formed a new company with his son Eugen on 9 June 1906, called C Benz Söhne. By 1908, it had turned to car production after demand for the gas engines they were building fell. This particular business, based in Ladenburg, to the east of Mannheim, was duly handed over to Eugen and his younger brother, Richard, in 1912. However, with the problems associated with the German economy following the First World War, the firm officially stopped building cars in 1923.

Benz & Cie AG continued down a safe path with its vehicle line-up, with a racing programme, diesel engine and aero-engine development going on in the background. The Benz badge gained its laurel wreath in the summer of 1909, and a take-over of Süddeutsche Automobilfabrik Gaggenau GmbH not long after provided Benz with a ready-made line of commercial vehicles.

Meanwhile, Hans Nibel had been put in charge of car design from 1910. Interestingly, Nibel's own love of racing (he'd been involved with the machine that formed the basis for the 'Blitzen Benz' record breaker) spawned a number of competition cars, and the Benz marque duly found favour with a wealthy clientele. One of the most ardent supporters of the brand was Prince Henry of Prussia – the brother of Kaiser Wilhelm II.

Benz introduced its first six-cylinder powerplant in 1914. This was actually an aero-engine, but the company stuck almost exclusively to straight-sixes for its road cars following the First

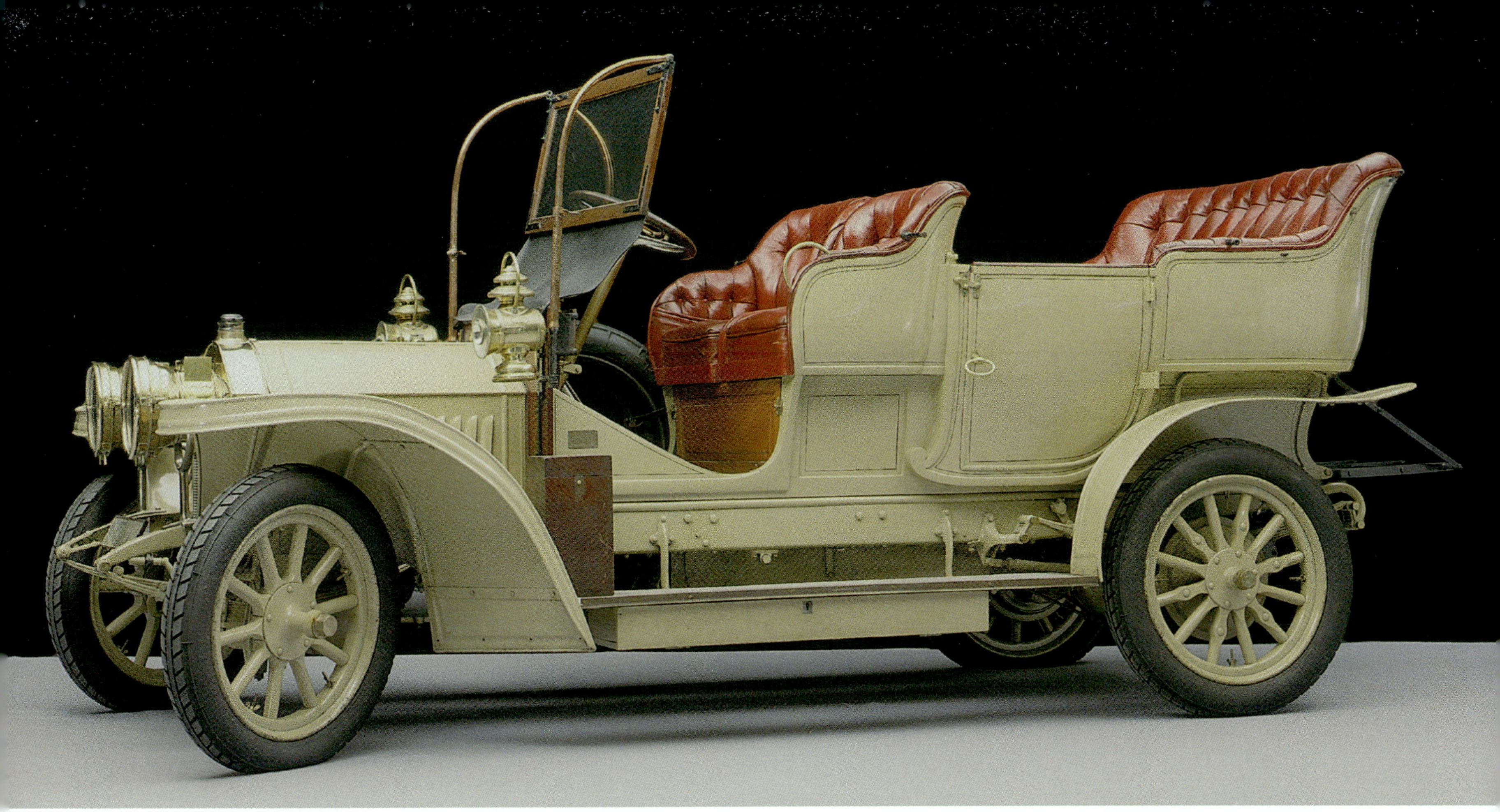

The shaft-driven 12/14hp Benz Parsifal from 1903.

Benz production in 1910.

A six-cylinder Benz 11/40hp Runabout of 1925 vintage.

World War. During the war years, Benz had produced some magnificent aero-engines, including four-valve per cylinder units and a V12 prototype. It also emerged from the conflict as a leading light in the field of diesel technology.

The merger of two great houses

Following the end of the First World War, Germany suffered greatly at the hands of hyperinflation. Such conditions are naturally far from ideal for manufacturers of expensive goods, and with Deutsche Bank holding a huge amount of shares in both the Daimler Motoren Gesellschaft and Benz & Cie AG, it was decided that a syndicate be formed in order to save production costs. An agreement of mutual interest was duly signed on 1 May 1924, with a full merger and the birth of Daimler-Benz AG taking place on 28 June 1926.

Although the company was known as Daimler-Benz, the cars were marketed using the Mercedes-Benz name, with Mercedes

Domestic advertising from 1929, not that long after the merger of two of the greatest names in the German car industry, if not the world.

EVOLUTION OF THE THREE-POINTED STAR

This series of pictures shows the way in which this most famous of trademarks has evolved over the years.

Angemeldet 1909

Angemeldet 1916

Angemeldet 1909

Angemeldet 1926

Angemeldet 1921

The supercharged six-cylinder SS (27/140/200hp) chassis fitted with a magnificent cabriolet body by Carrozzeria Castagna of Milan.

officially losing the accents along the way. Only two Benz models made it into the Mercedes-Benz passenger car programme, and both were gone by 1927. A new badge, combining the Mercedes-Benz name, Benz laurels and the familiar three-pointed star had been registered soon after the merger.

There were straight-eights from October 1928, and following the departure of Ferdinand Porsche at the end of the year, Hans Nibel took over sole responsibility as the company's Chief Engineer; the pair had been sharing the post since the merger.

Despite the difficult financial climate left in the wake of the Wall Street Crash, the marque entered the mid-1930s with some magnificent creations, with the SS and SSK giving way to the 500K and 540K. By this time, the company was producing a range of vehicles that went from modest 1.3-litre saloons,

The Type 170V Roadster seen in a 1937 catalogue illustration. In reality, this car can be classed as an ancestor of the SLK.

with their NA four at the rear, all the way up to 7.7-litre supercharged eights with their glamorous coachbuilt bodies.

Meanwhile, 1934 had witnessed the debut of the first of the Silver Arrows – the ultra-modern W25 Grand Prix car. This was followed by a string of successful models that, combined with the might of the Auto Union team, put Germany at the forefront of the motorsport scene until the outbreak of the Second World War. Record breakers were also built, based on the GP cars, and brought the new Autobahn network into use in a rather unexpected fashion – the straight, level roads being perfect for the challenge to find the fastest man on Earth.

Following Hans Nibel's death in 1934, Max Sailer took over as the head of design and R&D. Sailer had been associated with the Stuttgart marque for decades, most visibly as a racing driver of note in the vintage era. During Sailer's watch, products as diverse as the 540K, the 170V and 170H, and the 260D (the world's first diesel series-production passenger car) are released. The factory also built the first batch of VW30 test vehicles during the spring of 1937 – the ancestors of the Volkswagen Beetle.

Then, of course, 1939 brought with it conflict, first in Europe, and then on a global scale. Virtually all the historic Untertürkheim factory had been destroyed during successive Allied bombing runs in November 1943 and September 1944. Other plants were either destroyed or badly damaged, too, making it difficult for Daimler-Benz to bounce back once the hostilities came to an end in 1945.

The immediate postwar years

Fritz Nallinger had been appointed Chief Engineer in 1940, taking over from Max Sailor. Having been in charge of commercial vehicle development since May 1935, he was already a trusted and highly-experienced member of the Daimler-Benz team, and therefore an ideal candidate for the job.

Manfred von Brauchitsch on his way to victory in the 1937 Monaco Grand Prix. The W125 he is driving is one of the cars that helped create the 'Silver Arrows' legend. The silver bodywork came about when Team Manager Alfred Neubauer ordered the white paint (Germany's traditional racing colour) to be removed to save weight!

The Sindelfingen works in 1950, with the prewar 170-series resurrected to get production rolling again after the conflict. The Sindelfingen site had originally been purchased during the Great War era to facilitate the building of aircraft and aero-engines.

Like so many manufacturers, Daimler-Benz warmed over some of its prewar designs as part of the rebuilding process, releasing its first postwar car (ignoring utilitarian versions and commercial vehicles) in July 1947 – the bread-and-butter 1.7-litre 170V four-door sedan. By October that year, 1000 had been built, but commercials and repair work dominated the scene in Stuttgart as the transition from military to civilian production took place.

Research and development work recommenced in the middle of 1948. Soon after, the Unimog was unveiled, and car production reached 1000 units a month. Granted, it was still less than half the figure posted in the years leading up to the war, but for Dr Wilhelm Haspel, the company's Chairman, it must have seemed like a definite and most welcome sign of imminent recovery.

Two new 170-series variants (the 170S and 170D) joined the line-up in May 1949, and production continued until 1955, by which time the 180 had been introduced as a stablemate. The 170V and 170D were revised in June 1950, receiving, among other things, more powerful engines. Their popularity helped Daimler-Benz breeze towards a landmark figure of 50,000 postwar passenger cars built in October that same year.

Safety considerations were already starting to play an important role in vehicle development at Daimler-Benz. Karl Wilfert (in charge of body development at the Sindelfingen plant) filed a patent for a safety door lock in 1949, and Bela Barenyi

The 300SL prototype that was displayed at the 1954 International Motor Sports Show in New York.

came up with the passenger safety cell in 1951. In principle, both of these inventions are still in use to this day.

1951 witnessed the revival of six-cylinder engines with the launch of the 2.2-litre 220 series (W187) and the 3-litre 300 (W186 II) models unveiled in Frankfurt in the latter half of April. The 300 quickly picked up the 'Adenauer' nickname, as the German Chancellor, Konrad Adenauer, was a staunch supporter of the model and was rarely seen in public without one. The sporting two-door 300S (W188) made its debut later in the year at the Paris Salon.

The 170-series was updated again in 1952, with new models augmenting revised ones, but the debut of the 300SL sports-racer was perhaps the most telling sign that Daimler-Benz was back, its reputation being restored in the showrooms and on the track. A convincing win at Le Mans was followed by a deal with Max Hoffman, which secured a good sales outlet for Mercedes-Benz cars in America. Incidentally, Hoffman also handled Porsche, VW, Alfa Romeo and Jaguar imports for the US.

September 1953 marked the arrival of the slab-sided 'Ponton' series, giving the styling cue for a whole new generation of Mercedes-Benz models. It was launched in 1.8-litre four-cylinder guise (W120), but a 2.2-litre six-cylinder version (W180) had joined the line-up by the following spring as a replacement for the W187 model.

A Mercedes-Benz dealership in Wiener Neustadt, with a couple of 'Ponton' models each side of a 190SL. The 'Ponton' line, which had originally made its debut in 1953, featured modern styling, and was the first Mercedes-Benz to adopt unit body construction.

Mercedes-Benz made its long-awaited return to Grand Prix racing in 1954 with the 2.5-litre, normally-aspirated W196 model, fielded with both streamlined and open-wheeled bodies. Regulations at the time allowed sports-racers to be developed from GP cars, and Daimler-Benz responded with the 300SLR (or W196S, seen here) for use in the 1955 World Sports Car Championship. After some stunning performances, the curtain came down on the racing programme on 24 October 1955.

On the sporting front, 300SL and 190SL prototypes made their debut at a show in New York in early 1954, in the same year as the W196 Grand Prix car hit the tracks. As expected, it was a winner straight out of the box, and continued to dominate wherever it went in the following season, too. Domination with the 300SLR in the 1955 Mille Miglia was sadly overshadowed by the Le Mans disaster, where many spectators died following a freak accident, and Mercedes withdrew from racing soon after. A second magnificent era in motorsport had come to an end.

In the meantime, Daimler-Benz of North America Inc was founded in Delaware on 7 April 1955 to handle US imports. With so many new models coming in 1956, such as the 190, 219 and 220S, the timing couldn't have been better. Interestingly, though, in April 1957 (the month after the 300SL Roadster made its debut), a deal was struck with the Curtiss-Wright concern, and the Studebaker-Packard Corporation took on responsibility for the sales of Mercedes-Benz cars and diesel engines in the States. A subsidiary of Studebaker-Packard called Mercedes-Benz Sales Inc (MBS) was duly formed in August 1958, although this fell by the wayside at the start of 1965, when Mercedes-Benz of North America Inc (MBNA) took over US operations.

Back in Germany, the car range was overhauled in time for the 1958 Model Year, and during that sales season, power-assisted steering and seatbelts became an option long before the latter became a legal requirement. Other safety-minded introductions included a new wedge-pin door lock and a proper crash test programme, which began in earnest at the tail-end of 1959.

Ironically, considering they were bitter rivals in prewar racing, Daimler-Benz acquired a majority interest in Auto Union during 1958. In the following year, plans to take a stake in BMW were thwarted, although the remaining shares in Auto Union were secured at the end of 1959. The company was eventually sold to Volkswagen in 1964, signalling a revival of the Audi name (one of the four firms brought together under the Auto Union marque), later merging it with NSU. Today, Auto Union is ably represented by Audi AG, its cars carrying the same four rings on their noses as the prewar racers designed by Professor Ferdinand Porsche after he moved from the Mercedes camp. Audi is still owned by the VW group, which has since merged with Porsche. It's a small world in the German car industry!

Meanwhile, September 1958 brought with it a new fuel-injected 220SE (W128) model. Success in the field of long-distance rallying took the place of victories on the track, and success in the showrooms is easy to quantify with annual production averaging, by this time, around 100,000 units a year, plus around 55,000 commercial vehicles to add to this total.

The modern era

The 1959 Frankfurt Show heralded a new era for Daimler-Benz, with the first of the 'Fintail' series models lining up alongside a revised four-cylinder 'Ponton' line. These original 'Fintail' cars (W111) were six-cylinder saloons, replacing the 'Ponton' sixes, although by 1961, two-door fixed head and drophead models had been launched (with disc brakes and an automatic transmission adding technical appeal), as well as a new W110 four-cylinder range, bringing the 'Ponton' era to an end, and a flagship W112 3-litre model. The 'Fintail' variants were a perfect blend of modernity and tradition, and allowed Mercedes to make huge steps forward in the field of safety – the introduction of crumple zones being a case in point.

The SL range was also brought up-to-date during 1963, when the 230SL (W113) replaced the 190SL and 300SL, bridging the gap between the two in many ways, but the modern styling was another sign that the Mercedes-Benz brand had moved on a generation. Similar lines were chosen for the upmarket 1964 V8-engined 600 – a stately vehicle available as a 5/6-seater or 7/8-seater on an extended wheelbase.

Things moved forward again in September 1965, when the W108 and W109 models replaced the 'Fintail' six-cylinder saloons, although the two-door models and four-cylinder W110 line continued for a while longer, duly joined by the 250SL before augmenting the 280SL and a new range of '/8' machines that took the place of the 'Fintail' fours at the start of 1968. These W114 and W115 cars were a thoroughly modern interpretation

Advertising from 1961, featuring a Benz Patent and a 'Fintail' saloon, first introduced at the 1959 Frankfurt Show.

A piece of British advertising for the 230SL, released soon after its success on the 1963 Spa-Sofia-Liège Rally.

The Wankel-engined C111 about to go on test, with a 300SEL 3.5 saloon off to the right. The 6.3-litre version of the W109 saloon made a lasting impression on the tracks.

of traditional Mercedes thinking, overseen by Dr Hans Scherenberg, who took over the responsibility for product development following the retirement of Professor Fritz Nallinger at the end of 1965. As 1968 continued, the 300SEL 6.3 broke cover, along with an attractive W114 coupé body, which eventually went into production during the following year.

The 3.5-litre V8 engine made its debut at the 1969 Frankfurt Show, powering 300SEL 3.5 (W109) and two-door W111 variants, although the event was probably best remembered for the world premiere of the Wankel-engined C111. This magnificent creation was perhaps too far ahead of its time, although it's a shame that more wasn't done with the rotary engine – after a few more C111 prototypes, as with so many companies that had paid NSU for patent rights, the RE adventure came to an end.

In 1970, Hermann J Abs resigned as Chairman of the Daimler-Benz AG Supervisory Board, handing the reins to Franz Heinrich Ulrich. A few months later, Dr Joachim Zahn was made Chairman of the Board of Management, while the Hanomag truck concern became a wholly-owned subsidiary of the Stuttgart giant (the tractor side of the business was separated and sold to Massey Ferguson).

The 280SE 3.5 and 280SEL 3.5 saloons were added to the W108 series in early 1971, although it was the R107 SL that stole the limelight. Introduced in April, the two-seater V8 roadster was joined by a slightly longer tin-top version (the C107, or SLC) at the end of the year. Not long after, a new batch of W114 models joined the range, giving Mercedes-Benz a particularly sporting ambience in time to compliment the luxury W116 S-Class, announced at the 1972 Paris Salon. Eventually, 4.5-litre V8 engines were added to the S-Class

A German advert from the end of 1973 featuring a '/8' saloon in the foreground, a C107 SLC model to the left, and a W116 S-Class saloon in the background.

and SL line-up, as well as long-wheelbase variants on the big saloons.

Mercedes-Benz UK Ltd was formed as 1974 dawned, the same year in which the SL line gained a six-cylinder engine option, while 1975 saw the launch of the 450SEL 6.9 – a true wolf in sheep's clothing. With a workforce of roughly 150,000 at this time, annual production during 1975 stood at 350,098 cars and 229,302 trucks.

Tranquillity

After years of running countless model variations alongside each other – some, like the W111 two-door models, lasting six years beyond their four-door counterparts – the introduction of the W123-series saloons in January 1976 brought with them a sense of calm. Although a few of their '/8' predecessors were allowed to continue for a little while longer, compared with other model changeovers, it was a clean progression. From this point on, the W123s would take up the mid-range (as what would become known as the E-Class), the saloon, coupé and estate models augmenting the S-Class saloons at the top of the line, and the SL/SLC sports cars.

By now, Dr Wilfried Guth was at the helm of the Supervisory Board, and one of his first decisions was to make the new estate version of the W123 at the Bremen plant – first established by Borgward in 1938, but inherited by Daimler-Benz after the Hanomag takeover. This gradual move from commercial vehicle to passenger car production would duly become significant for fans of Mercedes sports cars at the end of the 1980s.

At the end of 1977, an all-alloy V8 was introduced on the 450SLC 5.0, while at the other end of the scale, a turbo-diesel engine was launched for the 300SD saloon. On 14 October that year, the 5,000,000th postwar passenger car left the line at Sindelfingen. Interestingly, the first million cars built after the conflict had taken 16 years to complete, whilst this last batch of a million had taken just two years. A few weeks later, Hans Scherenberg retired, leaving Werner Beritschwerdt in charge of product development.

Daimler-Benz had first toyed with ABS brake systems in 1970, but they ultimately became available in December 1978. Two months later, the long-running G-Wagen off-roader (Mercedes' answer to the Range Rover) was introduced, originally developed as a joint-project with Steyr-Daimler-Puch.

The supremely elegant W126 S-Class series was introduced at the 1979 Frankfurt Show, powered by 2.8-litre straight-sixes, or all-alloy 3.8- and 5.0-litre V8s. Production began on the state-of-the-art lines at Sindelfingen in December, which is when Joachim Zahn retired, allowing Dr Gerhard Prinz to become the new Chairman of the Board of Management of Daimler-Benz AG.

The W123 and SL/SLC models inherited new engines in 1980, and the availability of ABS brakes became more widespread. Airbags and seatbelt pretension systems became listed in the following year, keeping Daimler-Benz very much at the forefront of safety innovation and technology. 1981 also saw the last of the 600s built, as well as the first of the W126 coupés – the 380SEC and 500SEC ranking as one of the author's all-time favourites from the postwar era, even though they brought about the end of the SLC series.

This range shot from 1982 shows (from left to right) the W123 in saloon, estate and coupé guise, the S-Class in saloon and coupé guise, the SL sports car, and the G-Wagen off-roader. Not long after, the W201-series rounded off the line-up.

An all-new compact car, the 190/190E (W201), was announced in November 1982, bringing forth a predecessor to today's C-Class. A diesel-powered 190D was added in 1983, along with a high-performance 16v model, which managed to claim a number of world speed records a few weeks before it was launched.

With the death of Gerhard Prinz, Professor Werner Beritschwerdt stepped up to take on the Chairman's role, while Dr Rudolf Hörnig took over as head of R&D in May 1984. Catalytic converters became an option in Germany soon after, while particulate filters were employed on diesel cars, pointing the way for others to follow in a world that suddenly became aware of the 'Green' side of automotive engineering.

The respected W123-series was replaced by a new line of W124 models at the end of 1984, with styling closely resembling that of the W201. When the 1985 Frankfurt Show opened its doors for business, all three lines – the C-Class, E-Class and S-Class (including the SL) – had been face-lifted, and new technologies, such as ASD (an automatic locking differential), ASR (an early form of traction control) and 4MATIC (an automatic four-wheel drive system) had been presented to the public. Rightfully proud of its traditional engineering, Daimler-Benz had shown it was capable of moving with the times, taking advantage of the latest electronics wizardry.

W124-based coupés were introduced at the 1987 Geneva Show, and Edzard Reuter replaced Werner Beritschwerdt in the Chairman's office a few months later. At the same time, at the 1987 Frankfurt Show, new diesel engines were announced for W201 and W124 series cars, and the W126 series was given uprated V8 engines.

The Sauber-Mercedes C9 Group C car of 1988. The following race season marked the true return of the 'Silver Arrows' in more ways than one.

1988 brought with it news of Mercedes-Benz officially returning to motorsport, with a Group A programme, and a prestigious Group C one, building on the success of the Swiss Sauber team. Swapping black paint for silver, the Group C cars were in form from the off in the following season, taking the WSPC title with ease in 1989, and then again in 1990.

Enhancing the marque's new-found sporting image, the technologically-advanced R129 SL was launched at the 1989 Geneva Show, powered by pair of 3-litre straight-sixes or a 5-litre V8. There was also a 190E 2.5-16 Evolution announced at the event, produced as a 500-off homologation special to further the chances of the top Group A racing teams (an Evo II was built in 1990).

With so many different interests in a wide range of companies, Daimler-Benz AG was restructured in mid-1989, with Professor Werner Niefer named as Chairman of the Board of Management for the Mercedes-Benz AG wing. A face-lifted W124-series was announced soon after, and by the spring of 1990, all Mercedes passenger cars were powered by fuel-injected engines to give cleaner emissions.

Professor Hartmut Weule took over as the R&D boss in September 1990, and in the following month, closer ties were forged with AMG (the famous tuning company), and the 500E was introduced as the flagship of the W124 range, duly built at the Porsche factory in the Zuffenhausen district of Stuttgart.

The W140 S-Class made its debut at the 1991 Geneva Show, with 3-, 4-, 5- and 6-litre powerplants, the latter being an exotic V12. By the autumn, a large range of AMG models had joined the fray, as well as a four-seater convertible based on the W124 series (officially going on sale in the summer of 1992), and a C112 experimental sports car with a 'gullwing' body configuration.

The R129-type SL pictured at the time of its launch.

Mercedes officially withdrew from racing at the end of 1991, but new S-Class coupés were announced at the 1992 Detroit Show in January, and work continued on alternative fuel units in the background. The 600SL kept up the momentum, followed by a revised engine line-up for the W124 and W140 models later in the year.

A replacement for the 190 – the W202 C-Class – was launched in mid-1993, bringing with it a new form of model designation. The recently-released 600SL became the SL600 overnight as a result, but it was timely for the new engines adopted on the six-cylinder SLs, and the face-lifted W124s, which were correctly termed as E-Class models. It was all-change in the administration offices, too, with Helmut Werner named as the new Chairman of the Board of Management at Mercedes-Benz AG.

September 1993 brought with it a concept that duly became the A-Class, new AMG models, and a revised G-Wagen, keeping the off-roader alive and well. Then, in November, the company announced it was taking a stake in Britain's Ilmor Engineering, which signalled a wish to enter the Formula One and Indycar arena.

More S-Class and E-Class variants put in an appearance at the 1994 Geneva Show in March, but it was the Turin Show, which opened a month later, that held the most interest for sports car fans, as that was where the SLK prototype made its debut.

Many companies talk of having pedigree. However, with so many landmark machines to its name and a rich history created by some of the biggest names in the industry, it's fair to say that few can match the bloodlines behind the Mercedes-Benz brand …

2

BIRTH OF THE R170 SLK

The idea of selling a smaller, lighter and less expensive open sports car alongside the flagship SL was nothing new at Daimler-Benz, as the 190SL had been marketed as a stablemate for the 300SL in the late fifties and early sixties. With Mercedes model lines expanding at a good rate of knots, and the contemporary SL becoming more and more exclusive in a market suddenly awash with cheaper convertibles, the time was right to revive the concept ...

Things move quickly in the motoring world, even with today's longer development lead times. There was a period when America was buying every lightweight sports car England could produce, with the likes of MG, Triumph, and Jaguar, to name but a few, having a captive audience and a market share that only the Italians seemed able to challenge. By the start of the seventies, though, the scene was a very different one. In their infinite wisdom, the powers that be in the States had mooted a ban on convertibles, saying they were unsafe, and while the legislation was never passed, the very idea sent shock waves throughout the industry.

In Britain, we only need to look at the Triumph TR7 and Jaguar XJ-S to see what the outcome was. Both were ultimately converted into dropheads, but these were never as good as the coupés they were derived from. In Italy, everything new from the mainstream manufacturers had a tin-top, and Germany hedged its bets with Porsche making the Targa, and Mercedes-Benz introducing a close-coupled SLC coupé to run alongside the SL, just in case. Even Japan had to rethink its strategy, with the Fairlady convertibles evolving into the Datsun 240Z coupé, although, ironically, this was probably a useful turning point in the history of Japanese companies making it big in the States.

As we limped into the middle of the eighties, with oil shocks and bad management bringing a lot of the industry to its knees, there was hardly any choice for open car fans, at least in the

Dr Dieter Zetsche, without whom there would probably be no SLK. It was his push to revive a sidelined project that breathed life into the small convertible programme.

mass-produced arena. The Alfa Romeo Spider kept soldiering on, but was starting to show its age; the Fiat Spider was continued with Pininfarina badging; the Mercedes SL had gone unchanged for over a decade, and after that it was a few Yank Tanks and a handful of quirky British machines that made up the majority of off-the-shelf convertible models on offer.

As the industry's hierarchy increasingly became dominated by accountants and marketing men with no love for cars and no feel for what was needed in the showroom, happy to continue selling grey machines that were safe bets, the convertible slipped even further from favour, as this new breed of industry leaders could point to low sales figures to justify their low-risk appetite. The fact that you can't sell what isn't there didn't occur to them, and it took the Japanese to reinvent the lightweight sports car, or LWS. After launching the MX-5 Miata in February 1989, Mazda provided enthusiasts with the car they'd been waiting for. It was a huge hit, with over 100,000 selling by the end of 1990.

Mazda's act of bravery resulted in a rush of activity in Europe as others jumped on the bandwagon: basking in the nostalgia of one generation and the newfound wealth of another. Lotus pitched a new Elan; Alfa Romeo launched a face-lifted Spider to keep things going until an all-new model could be announced in 1994; Fiat introduced the Barchetta in the following year when the BMW Z3 was also released, riding on the Z1's tailcoats, by which time both the MG and AC names had been revived via open cars, and Porsche made it known that a two-seater convertible christened the Boxster was in the pipeline. Perhaps not surprisingly, given the way they had been filling in the gaps at entry level, in the background, the designers and engineers at Daimler-Benz were hard at work on their own compact open car …

The dream

The need to shower shareholders with healthy profits is always at the front of any thoughts on new model lines, so the W201 (and later, the C-Class) was launched to fill the gap beneath the bread-and-butter E-Class, and then a green light was given for the development of the A-Class as soon as the marketplace revealed a desire for something even smaller. But car designers tend to be an enthusiastic bunch, and the opportunity to work on a sports car is usually considered the ultimate perk of the job – a chance to release all those swoopy lines bottled up inside. With the figures now proving the sports car market existed to even the most removed of bean counters, the green light was

One of the earliest SLK design proposals, this one dating from August 1989. Incidentally, the 'SLK' designation was thought up by Günther Ellenrieder, one of the designers at the Sindelfingen plant.

Another sketch from the 'dream' era – a lot less ostentatious than the previous drawing and doubtless attractive, but still lacking that certain distinctive Mercedes look.

Even though the SLK project had been shelved, designers continued producing images of their dream sports car. This sketch is dated July 1991, and perhaps shows a touch of frustration, as it was obvious that something like this would not really be in keeping with the Stuttgart company's image.

Two more drawings from 1991; the red car nicely incorporating the 'Variodach' roof, and evoking memories of the past with its blisters over the wheelarches.

given for a small convertible, and, for a select few under Bruno Sacco (the Italian-born Chief Designer at Mercedes since the mid 1970s, duly appointed as head of styling in 1993, with about 300 workers under him), the dream became a reality.

Inspired by the wave of admiration and passion created by the Mazda MX-5, Dr Wolfgang Peter (head of passenger car development since 1985) had requested a series of design proposals for a compact two-seater open car suitable to carry the hallowed three-pointed star on its nose. The SLK concept was pretty much an application of Bauhaus school of design thinking, with Walter Gropius once stating that "a modern automobile should be technically mature, attractive and inexpensive."

Although these words had been uttered before the Second World War, they were still applicable, especially the part on pricing if one wanted to attract larger sales than the contemporary SL was garnering. Conquest sales would be the key to a successful project, and one area of the marketplace thus far broadly untapped by the Stuttgart giant was the youth market – the majority of younger buyers had been left drooling at showroom windows at the two-seater creations ever since the 190SL had been dropped from the line-up in 1963, as pricing moved further upwards and further out of reach.

An interesting tail treatment in this 1992 sketch, but it was way off the mark in the eyes of the selection committee.

Armed therefore with a brief to design a compact, two-seat convertible, aimed at a younger audience than the traditional Mercedes-Benz clientele of the time – whilst still retaining typical styling cues that would instantly discern the car's brand – the first styling sketches were made in Professor Harald Leschke's newly-formed Advanced Design Department at Sindelfingen in 1989.

Leschke's team put together countless sketches in the space of a few months – some like those seen in the dreams of the designers (ultimately too far from expectations of a car carrying the Benz badge), some ultra-conservative and drawing on the past, and others somewhere in the middle that came much closer to fulfilling the requirements of the brief, and deserving of further investigation.

In time, no less than ten one-fifth scale models had been reviewed in detail, leading to the creation of two full-size clays in the early part of spring 1990. However, by the end of May that year, the project had been axed – doubtless a victim of the uncertain financial climate left in the wake of Black Monday. This is when the stock markets lost a huge amount of their value in October 1987, its fallout bringing about a temporary end to the so-called 'Yuppie' lifestyle and a short, sharp shock to providers of luxury goods.

The reality

In an unusually unsettled era by Stuttgart's standards, Dr Dieter Zetsche was appointed Chief Engineer in early 1992, with

A posed picture of Romuald Juraschek making sketches some time after a design freeze had been called on the SLK project. Juraschek was responsible for the interior of the 1994 Turin Show model, by the way.

Jürgen Hubbert in charge of the passenger car division. Zetsche took Dr Wolfgang Peter's place, who'd been moved sideways after the W140 project, which, while it had its fans, had run behind schedule and well over budget. Zetsche would later go on to become the head of Mercedes-Benz, but of far greater importance to SLK fans is the fact that one of his first decisions in his new role as Chief Engineer was to revive the compact sports car project.

As it happens, the dedicated team of 20 stylists had never given up hope on the project, and thumbing through sketches, one can see quite a few dated the tail-end of 1990 and even a number dating from 1991. As such, when Zetsche, with support from Werner Niefer at that time, gave the nod to revive the small convertible in the spring of 1992, there were already quite a few fresh proposals on the table, and a presentation of 15 one-fifth scale models was put together almost immediately. The number was quickly reduced to eight, which were then reviewed once more as soon as they had all been painted in silver to eliminate any advantage or disadvantage caused by different colouring. After all, the subtle way in which light interacts with the body

The eight one-fifth scale models selected for the next round of reviews in the spring of 1992. To make things fair, they were all painted in silver before the next lot of judging took place.

contours can make the difference between a design being interesting or totally lifeless, and darker colours always give a deeper lustre that creates stronger highlights.

Designing a dream sports car all sounds easy enough, but one has to remember that an important element of classic Mercedes design is its timeless appeal. One only needs to think of the Pagoda SL, or better still the R107-series that followed – how many other cars could run for so long yet still look contemporary? Think of the two-door W111 models, or the first SEC – masterpieces of design that have stood the test of time far better than most, simply because they were pure; free of the gimmicks and add-ons that quickly date a vehicle. Following fashion might make something popular for a little while, but to keep something in vogue over a long period of time (a must given the outrageous costs involved in creating a modern automobile), subtlety of line and a more conservative approach is called for. Add in the need to appeal to younger customers, as well as the safety and other engineering requirements that dictate bulk in areas designers would rather see lithe body panels, and one can see why the brief caused a good few sleepless nights for Leschke and the team in his charge.

Michael Mauer looking over the photo-boards that were produced when cutting the number of proposals under review from eight to five.

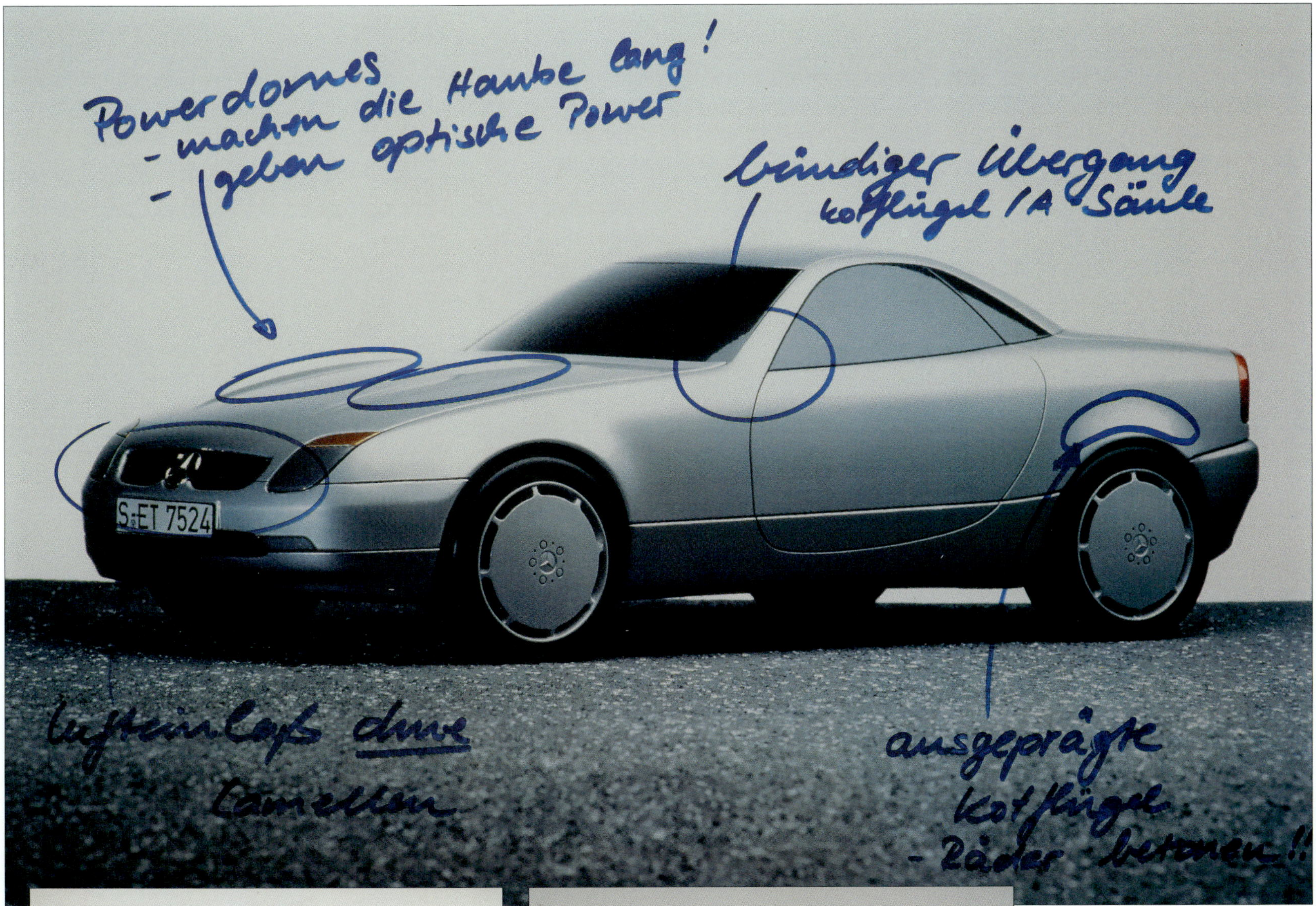

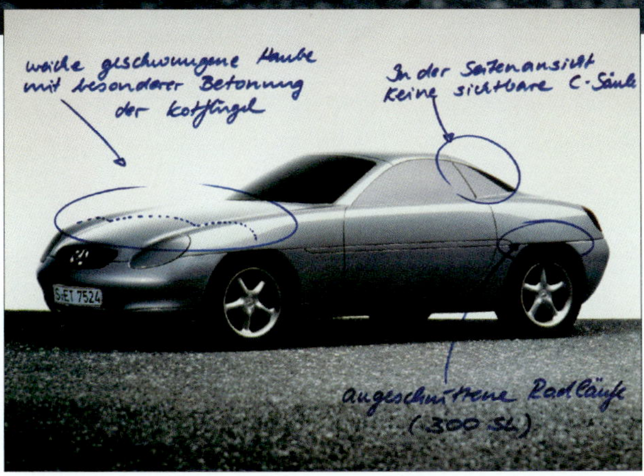

A selection of the photo-boards from 1992, complete with comments made by the design staff hierarchy. These were used to highlight strong and weak points in the design, to make progress to the next stage that much easier for all involved.

A close-up of Michael Mauer's winning model. Note the lighting arrangements and the drilled grille, which were features used for the show vehicles, and the bonnet bulges that conjured up an image of the 300SL road cars of yore. In recognition of his work on the SLK, Mauer was promoted to department head in 1995.

As with most of these projects from the larger manufacturers, the starting point is deciding which components to use for the drivetrain and suspension, as these determine a lot of the dimensions designers need to work within. With additional input from engineering staff on things like desired wheelbase and track measurements, it is then decided what panelwork could effectively be borrowed from existing models. After carefully reviewing what can and can't be used from the contemporary parts bin, then deciding what needs to be made specially in order to appease the engineers whilst keeping an eye on costs, a set of dimensions is eventually put forward by the planning department. Ultimately, the thoroughly-modern W202 C-Class

More angles to consider on the Mauer scale model, now with conventional door handles added to make it more realistic.

– finished on paper, but yet to find its way into the showrooms – was chosen to provide a lot of the donor parts, including a shortened version of the floorpan.

Working around a relatively short wheelbase length of 2400mm (94.5in), the same as that of the old 300SL and 190SL models from almost four decades before, and all the SLs that followed through to the end of the W113 run, all of the designs featured a hardtop, which would eventually be a rather unique piece of engineering in production form – an electrically-operated folding steel hardtop that provided all the benefits of a fixed-head coupé, but none of the bulk of a traditional hardtop, and the fun of a drophead at the flick of a switch.

Michael Mauer, one of the design team, stated: "There was more variation than normal in the early sketches. We tried a number of different themes, from rounded, retro-SL designs through to modern, hard-edged ones.

"By the time we started 3D versions, the proposals were more honest, with two fairly distinct avenues of thinking. The first was historic, with attempts to create a modern version of the old SL with rounded fenders and a feeling of the fifties, and the other was a modern approach, using details of the SL but taking the design a few steps forward.

"Simply doing a retro design didn't link up with our determination that the SLK should be a market leader for six or seven years. We wanted to combine a future-orientated shape with support design that reminded people of our history, such as the power bulges on the bonnet, and the SL-inspired face.

"We wanted more sporting proportions than the SL, so reduced the overhangs. The SL is our idea of an elegant sporting car. The SLK should look more youthful and dynamic."

By June 1992, five of the eight models (already whittled down from the 15 originals) had been selected by a small committee to be made full-size and looked at in greater detail. Jorg Prigl, who oversaw the SLK project in its early days, noted in 1996: "We felt the SLK's three most important elements were a youthful design, visible innovative technical features and a small size."

Eventually, after another round of reviews and a small breather to see what the opposition was doing at Porsche and BMW, a rubber stamp was put on the approved design – the one fielded by Michael Mauer – in March 1993. Considering the worrying financial climate at the time, with a decidedly slow recovery from the 1987 stock market crash, this was a very positive move, presumably because the marketing men wanted to make the most of the open car boom that was then in full-swing.

Luckily, at the end of May 1993, when Helmut Werner was named as the new Chairman of the Board of Management at Mercedes-Benz AG (taking over the reins from Werner Niefer), the SLK, duly given the R170 project code, was seen as the ideal tool to spearhead a fresh marketing drive planned by Werner and his team. "The SLK is in many ways symbolic of our company, which has become much faster-moving in recent years," he went on record saying. The car's future was guaranteed ...

THE 190SL: THE ORIGINAL SLK

Back in the 1950s, Mercedes was selling its race-inspired 300SL to a small group of connoisseurs, its size restricted not so much by desire, but by price. The bottom line is, the majority of car enthusiasts would have liked a 'Gullwing' SL in their garage, but at almost $9000 in the States (just $2000 shy of the average house price at the time), it was simply out of reach.

The marketing chaps were well aware of this fact, and equally aware of the kudos attached to the SL badge thanks to the competition exploits of the first 300SL model, which was a pure racer that won just about everything worth winning in Europe, as well as delivering a stirring performance in the Carrera Panamericana. As such, plans were laid for a more reasonably-priced SL to be sold alongside its 3-litre stablemate from the start.

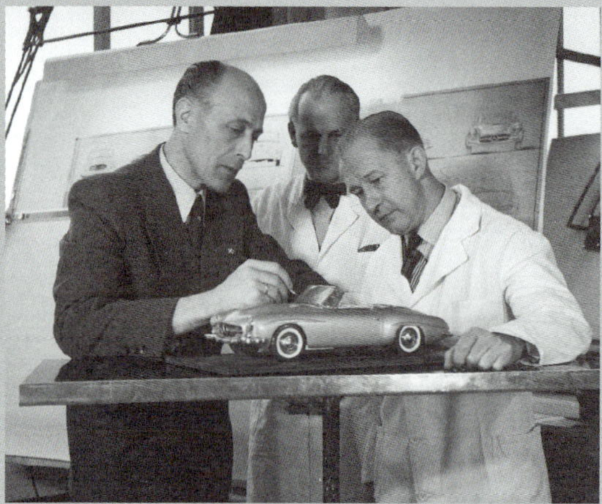

Walter Häcker (left) going over the final styling details on a scale model of the W121 190SL.

The pre-production prototype 190SL in the design studio, with a completely different bonnet profile to the car displayed in New York at the beginning of 1954 (the model closest to the wheel actually has the earlier type of bulge). The blister over the rear wheelarch was also added at the last minute.

The announcement of the two new Mercedes sports cars, in February 1954 at the International Motor Sports Show in New York, had enthusiasts in raptures: the 3-litre, fuel-injected 300SL with styling based on the 1953 SL prototype, and the much simpler, smaller-engined 190SL. Although it would be some time before either SL made it into the showrooms (the second Type W198 300SL, for instance, wasn't built until six weeks after the New York exhibition had ended, and even that was still a pre-production prototype), it was no coincidence that they were announced just as the latest W196 F1 car was about to hit the Grand Prix scene.

Series production of the 190SL convertible started in May 1955, about six months behind schedule. This was rather ironic, given that the 190SL was always going to provide Daimler-Benz with better volume sales in the States than the 300SL. However, people had an image of the Gullwing body whenever the SL moniker was mooted, hence the model release order, and the smaller car could then waft by on the fame of its bigger brother by using the same Sport Licht badge.

While it's fair to say the 300SL was built using many production parts sourced from the regular road car line, the ratio was much higher in the 190SL. Even the chassis was based on a shortened Type 180 pressed-steel floorpan rather than a dedicated tubular spaceframe, while most of the running gear and chassis components were simply lifted straight out of the Type 180 parts bins. This reduced cost and development time, with advantages far outweighing the disadvantages for the manufacturer.

Styled under the watchful gaze of Walter Häcker, the final prototype was exhibited at the Geneva Show in the spring of 1955. Compared with the 1954 show car, the bonnet, bumpers and lights were revised, and the grille and rear wings brought more into line with the 300SL, although the Ponton styling influence was still very much in evidence on the latter.

A hardtop was available from the off, giving the buyer the choice of a convertible roadster (with soft top only), or a car with a hardtop, supplied with or without a hood. Interestingly, the hardtop model was called a coupé in official paperwork, and came with additional chrome trim on the sills and wheelarch

Advertising announcing the arrival of the 190SL, aimed at American servicemen based in Germany.

blisters. Early hardtops were crafted from aluminium, but were made from pressed steel from the spring of 1956.

The body itself was largely all-steel on the 190SL, although the front and rear lids and door skins were aluminium. Even lighter doors were announced in the New York press material and appeared in several catalogues thereafter. These, along with the fitment of a lightweight aero-screen and removal of the bumpers helped reduce weight for those wishing to go racing at weekends.

On a more practical note, while the 300SL had next to nothing in the way of trunk space due to its oversized fuel tank, with a parcel shelf behind the seats providing the main luggage area, the 190SL had a good-sized boot. Fitted luggage was available from the maker for both cars. In addition, a third transverse jump-seat was

An early 190SL, initially priced at DM 16,500 in Germany. The later-style hardtop, introduced in October 1959, gave far better rearward visibility.

An early 190SL on the production line, with Gullwing models visible in the background.

Tail of the 1957 MY 190SL. It's actually easier to date a 190SL from the rear view: the larger rear lights seen here were introduced in June 1956, and, whilst always fitted to US cars, rear bumper guards became standard for all markets in July 1957, when they were modified to carry the number plate lights. The 1960 MY hardtop gives another clue, but about the only significant change applied after that was to the bootlid lock, which was separated from the lift in 1960.

listed for the 190SL, fitting in behind the two front ones, or a bench-style front seat was another option.

The engine was a high output 1897cc sohc four, with the same bore as the 300SL, but a shorter 83.6mm stroke. This bore/stroke combination was quite different to that of the original Type 180, adding 130cc to the cubic capacity, which had started out at 1767cc for the sedans, but it was duly adopted for the 1956 190 series, as well as the Type 180a of 1957 vintage. In the 190SL, a pair of twin-choke Solex carburetors and an 8.5:1 compression ratio gave 105bhp DIN at 5700rpm, with power taken to the rear wheels through a four-speed manual transmission.

Using the Type 180 floorpan allowed the Daimler-Benz engineers to employ the sedan's front subframe arrangement for the SL, with the engine, gearbox and front suspension system carried on an independent pressed-steel cradle that was then attached to the body via rubber mounts to isolate NVH – an incredibly advanced feature for the time. The concept was further refined in January 1956 thanks to an improvement in the way the engine was mounted in the subframe.

The 190SL may not have been quite as glamorous as the 300SL, but it was an accomplished sporting tourer that was infinitely more affordable to buy and run. The North American market was by far the most important outlet for European sports cars, of course, with the 190SL introduced to US buyers at a reasonable $3998.

A late 190SL with a W111 Fintail coupé in a dealership window.

The suspension itself was quite conventional, with fabricated upper and lower arms at the front, coil springs around damper units, and an anti-roll bar. The back end featured a low-pivot swing axle with the addition of revised, fairly hefty trailing links to give superior roadholding, the handling situation being further helped by the adoption of 13in wheels and tyres, which, although of unusually small diameter for the day, reduced the roll centre height.

Braking was via drums all-round, but with the drums themselves made from cast iron rather than the expensive Al-Fin bimetal (ribbed alloy sleeves over cast drums) items used on the 3-litre car. They were still finned, at least, for enhanced heat dissipation, while a servo was initially offered as an option before becoming standard shortly after production began. Steering, meanwhile, came via the familiar recirculating-ball system, for so long championed by the men in Stuttgart. Lhd or rhd was available, unlike the 300SL coupé, which was officially sold with left-hand drive only.

The 190SL was subjected to a number of detail changes over the years. By far the most important were carried out in time for the 1960 Model Year, when the engine's compression ratio was upped to 8.8:1 to maintain power output at 105bhp (120bhp SAE), and a new hardtop was introduced to give better visibility. A total of 25,881 190SLs had been built by the time production ended in February 1963.

The Mauer design

Michael Mauer, born in 1962 and now in charge of design at Porsche, had come up with a very mature proposal – its wedge shape giving a taller rear end that doubtless helped tip the balance in its favour. After all, one needed to consider the packaging of the folding roof mechanism, and that's something that would have proved difficult on at least four of the eight designs left under consideration in 1992 – assuming one wanted even a vestige of luggage space once the top was down. It's also probably fair to say that Mauer's model looked more like a roadster than a coupé, with its bold stance giving the car a purposeful attitude.

In some ways, with its sharp wedge profile, the Mauer design resembled the Maserati OPAC Spyder that had appeared at Turin in 1992, although typical attention to detail with a mass-market in mind was much in evidence, such as the large wraparound combination lights at the rear, doing away with a lot of variations for regional lighting regulations (or at least keeping them within a single housing), and fixed headlights that eliminated potential reliability problems. There was also a lot less muscle built into the wing lines, perfectly befitting a car that was designed to appeal to both sexes and a wide age group. Its styling was more playful than aggressive or elegant, but totally in keeping with what we have come to expect from Mercedes-Benz. It was a clean, functional design; very much in tune with Teutonic values.

At the front, the simple grille was self-framed, with the three-pointed star in its regular spot for sporting Benz models, but supported on a mount at the lower edge. The headlights were flush with the wing edges on the outside, and fairly narrow, allowing the grille to dominate, and had the indicators integrated into the top section. The large main grille allowed a narrow slit underneath the bumper line, and the bumper mouldings themselves were rounded at their extremities to aid aerodynamics, and make the car more manoeuvrable in tight parking spots. The bonnet was given a pair of power bulges like those seen on the W198 300SLs to provide an historical reference, one side having a duct to channel air into the engine bay, although this latter feature was not required on the production car.

From the side, the short overhangs made the design look more compact and sporty, but would also have a very positive affect on the handling of the real thing. Having such a long-wheelbase for so small a car also helped, pushing the wheels out closer to the corners. The leading edge of the front wing dropped into the same profile as the two-tone bumper moulding, leaving enough of the indicator unit exposed above it to do away with additional turn signal repeaters. The lower colour on the air dam was carried over to the side cladding and rear valance, the latter kicking upwards at the back to visually reduce the height of the rear flanks. Likewise, the use of the cladding and a lowered upper edge on the door helped prevent the design from looking too dumpy. The shutlines on the doors gave a sense of forward motion, matching the shape of the roof, which was kept as short and low as possible. The narrow quarter-light behind the door would help with rearward vision and lightened the look of the C-post, while the large rear light enclosure wrapped around the side, with one eye on regulations and another on balancing the overall design, which was decidedly heavier at the back than the front. The oversized wheels could never be used, of course, as costs would have escalated too much and ride quality would have to be compromised, but the wheelarch profiles above them were beautifully integrated, adding substance without resorting to gimmicks.

Moving around the back, while the attractive window graphics continued to impress, this was perhaps the weakest element of the proposal. The boot shutlines ran a long way out to the edges of the wing tops, and angled in slightly as they moved towards the bumper blade. The light clusters were like those of the W202 with extensions on the boot lid, the lower edge stopping short of the curve that mated the panelwork and the plain bumper. This large moulding, which hid the exhaust pipes, looked particularly heavy, although the number plate recess above it and the three-pointed star above that balanced things nicely, and a couple of swage lines helped break it up a bit.

The Turin Show car before it was given clear light lenses. It also had a leather-wrapped steering wheel at this time, although a carbonfibre one was made ready in time for the Italian event, which ran from 22 April to 1 May in 1994.

Turin teaser

Although the design and engineering work on the production car was almost finished – something deemed a necessity by modern automotive practice, with extensive testing followed by a lengthy lead-time for tooling and production facilities to be put in place – the company was eager to alert the world of its new baby. In fact, Mercedes was aiming to get 40,000 advance orders, which would mean two years of work guaranteed at the Bremen plant, and for this reason, there was already frank talk of a production car based on C-Class components, slated for 1996 production.

Serving as a teaser, the 'Studie SLK' was given a prime spot in a 1994 Turin Show display that beautifully portrayed the past, present and future of Mercedes sports cars. As Bruno Sacco commented at the time: "We have taken the opportunity offered by the Turin Motor Show to highlight the long-running role of Mercedes-Benz in industrial design and automotive culture, as well as the important part it has played in the evolution of the sports car."

The Turin car was actually quite faithful to the Mauer proposal, with a drilled aluminium sheet for the grille and the same headlight treatment – a modern interpretation of the front mask of the 1952 SL racers, with sharper, squared-off lines taking the place of the rounded shapes of the early fifties. The purity of the design and lack of bumpers reinforced the idea.

However, tiny driving lights had been added in the lower section of the air dam, the door shapes had been simplified for ease of production, and the rear light units (with clear lenses, like the indicators at the front of the car) were noticeably sharper, folding and tapering around the sides in such a way as to visually lighten the wing panel, as well as being a single piece, framing

The 'Studie SLK,' as it appeared at the 1994 Turin Show.

the angled boot lid. The twin exhaust pipes were exposed in a recess in the rear valance, but perhaps the biggest difference was the use of twin fairings to cover the roll-over hoops behind the seats, evoking memories of Moss and 'Jenks' and their 300SLR in winning form on the 1955 Mille Miglia. The 17-inch, five-spoke alloys, shod with 225/45 ZR-rated Pirelli rubber up front and 235/45s on the back, were definitely a tip of the hat to modernity.

The two-tone black and red interior was also a striking combination of the new and the traditional. The lightweight T-shaped dashboard featured exposed instrument binnacles for a sporty look, in much the same way as the Porsche Boxster prototype displayed at the 1993 Detroit Show, although that car, too, would have a lot of interior details toned down before production. The silver gauge faces, plus flashes of chrome and polished alloys hinted at days of yore, opposing carbonfibre on the steering wheel, instrument backing and inner door handles. There were bare panels in the footwells and on large swathes of the doors to add a sporting flavour, along with drilled pedals. There was even a hint of tartan check in the seat inserts to remind

Unlike so many concept cars, the 'Studie SLK' could actually be driven. The company even let a few selected journalists loose in it, guaranteeing exposure of the car well beyond the show coverage from Italy.

folks of the various Mercedes racers from the fifties. The oval rearview mirror was a nice retro touch, matching the shape of the door mirrors, while the seatbelts and dual airbags, as well as a full heating and ventilation (HVAC) setup and other fully functional systems, pointed to a near-production status.

It has to be said, the timing couldn't have been better to launch a sports car. The end of March had witnessed the company's first involvement in Formula One for four decades, as an engine supplier to the Sauber team at this stage, and a couple of months later, Al Unser Jr won the prestigious Indianapolis 500 in the States with a Penske-Mercedes PC23.

Although there was no roof on the SLK at this time, there were already strong hints regarding the power top and even mechanical specifications. Indeed, little was done to hide the fact that this was a car headed for the showrooms, with preliminary forecasts of it being available in 1996, eventually hitting the UK in 1997, priced at around £24,000.

To keep the attention of the press, a few selected journalists were allowed to drive the car, powered at the time by a 150bhp 2.2-litre NA engine linked to a five-speed manual transmission, although there was already mention of a 200bhp supercharged version to further whet the appetite. The marketing men had suddenly moved into overdrive promoting this machine!

Sporting colour-keyed door handles (they had been black earlier on), the Turin Show car was tested by *Classic & Sports Car* for its November 1994 issue. It noted: "[When you see the car] in the flesh for the first time, nothing prepares you for a Benz that looks so diminutive on the road. It's virtually the same length as a Mazda MX-5, but the heavily wedge-shaped body has real presence and elegance.

"On the road, this car feels almost production ready. Body rigidity is outstanding, and I was never aware of scuttle shake or body tremor. The steering is light and the short wheelbase endows the car with a very tight turning circle. Best of all is a lack of wind roar, at least up to 70mph. It's clear that Mercedes has done a lot of work to ensure that the SLK suffers few of the usual drawbacks of open motoring."

Furthermore, some clever wording from Dieter Futschik, who led the show-car project, left the mouths of enthusiasts watering in anticipation. "Many of the details will be different," he noted in the summer of 1994, "but 99 per cent of the spirit will be carried over. [The SLK will be] a car with its own strong image and personality."

MERCEDES-BENZ DESIGNATIONS

For many years, Mercedes-Benz models have been identified by a vehicle class letter (or series of letters) and a number, which usually relates to an engine size. It's a system that has continued to this day, with C 350 being a C-Class saloon with a 3.5-litre power-unit, although the engine displacements don't always tie-up precisely in the way they used to.

The designation that interests us the most at this stage in the story, however, is 'SL,' as in 190SL, and so on. The '190' denotes a 1.9-litre powerplant, while 'SL' is short for Sport und Licht – in English, this would translate into a description of a lightweight sports (LWS) model.

For reference, the addition of an 'R' suffix (to make SLR) distinguished the 300SLR sports-racer from the 3-litre 300SL production road cars, while a 'C' (to make SLC) denotes a coupé version of the SL, introduced in the 1970s.

One will also come across a 'K' quite often in Mercedes circles, which used to refer to short chassis models in prewar days (as in Kurz), but nowadays is usually taken to mean Kompressor, the German for supercharger. Having said that, the SLK model was sold in normally-aspirated and supercharged guise using the same SLK moniker for both vehicle types. We can therefore safely say that in the case of the R170, the SLK designation stands for a shortened version of the SL.

The Vario roof

There's nothing new about power tops, even metal folding ones. They've been around for more than half a century, and even longer if one considers some of the limited production models that were around in the 1930s. However, despite undoubted benefits, the concept never really took off, mainly due to the space the mechanism took up, as well as the cost involved, which limited applications.

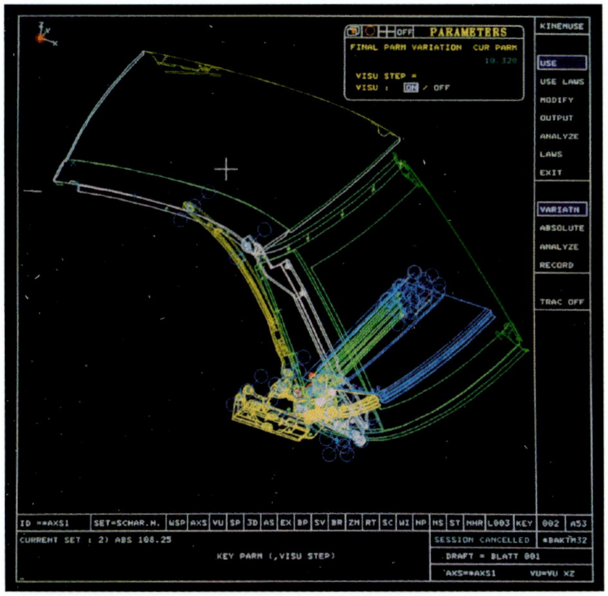

The fully automatic, power-operated 'Variodach' folding steel top was an extremely advanced piece of engineering that, perhaps not surprisingly, took several years to perfect. Making the two-piece top drop away into the boot was one thing, but it also had to leave room for luggage once it was folded.

Anyone who has run an open car for any length of time – the author included – will know that cloth tops are difficult to keep clean, and plastic rear windows are a real pain, especially as they age. The more modern top materials still have their problems in very cold weather, and glass rear windows, whilst being more practical, rule out the option of quarter lights (which go a long way towards improving rearward visibility) and tend to enlarge the receiving box needed for the hood to fold properly. In addition, storing a hardtop can present another concern during the summer months, particularly when they weigh as much as an old Mercedes one! From a design point of view, there is the difficult balance between the requirements of the mechanism and aesthetics to consider, as well as soundproofing and resistance to fluttering.

None of these points were lost on the engineers and planners at Daimler-Benz, and from the start, back in 1989, there were already thoughts of a metal folding roof, not only to add practicality to the package, but also

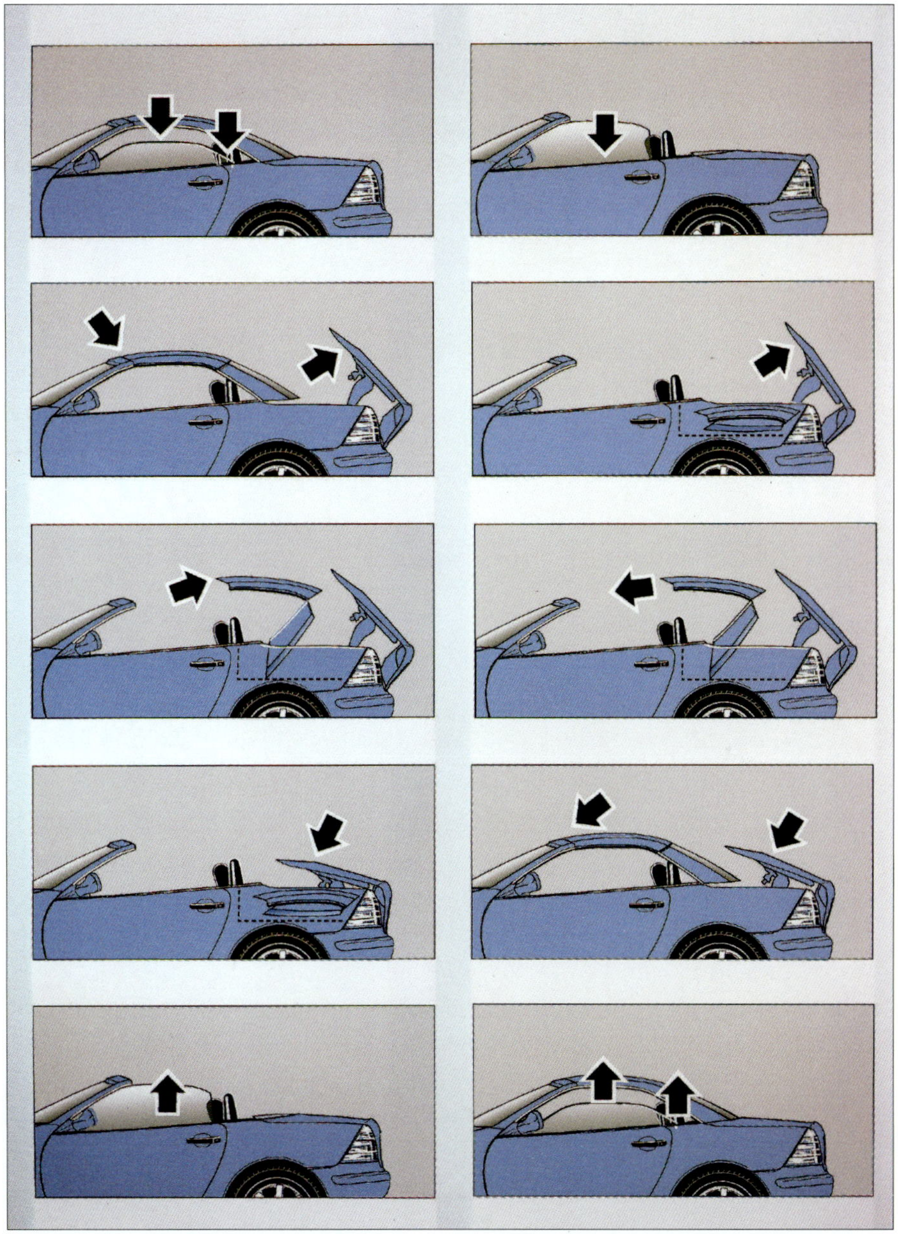

The opening sequence of the fully-lined 'Variodach' can be seen in the left-hand set of images, while those on the right-hand side show the closing sequence. It was all made possible by hinges on the forward and trailing edges of the bootlid, allowing the panel to act as a cover for the roof and a conventional bootlid giving access to the luggage compartment at the same time. There were no catches to release or anything else: a single button took care of everything. Note also the way in which the windows rise and fall automatically to avoid damage to the side seals.

The 'Variodach' top in action. The roof could be dropped or raised in 25 seconds at the touch of a button; a manual back-up system was also installed. Having tested the roof to be reliable for a minimum of 20,000 cycles, though, it would only really be in the event of a battery being discharged that one would need the manual back-up.

distance the car from its competitors by offering something new and worthwhile.

Development work on the so-called 'Variodach' had actually started before the R170 project was even thought of, as a team of Sindelfingen body designers led by Arno Jambor had already begun developing a metal folding roof with the R129 SL in mind as early as 1986. After all, manually-operated soft-tops were only just acceptable on the R107-series SLs, meaning all sorts of power hoods had to be investigated for its successors. By the middle of 1989, with Walter Treser having recently brought the idea back into the mind of the public via his T1 Roadster, Jambor and his team were able to demonstrate a prototype roof that was compact enough not to take up all the luggage space in a car, and with Wolfgang Peter requesting proposals for a small convertible coming through at the same time, the idea blossomed, with the new top being considered an integral part of the design. Even when the original SLK project was cancelled, work on the innovative roof continued, with something resembling the final 'Variodach' appearing in 1991.

As soon as the SLK moved from dream to reality status, development on the roof was handed over to production specialists, with Jürgen Schrader and Klaus Bernhard Schenk leading the way. Making the concept work was one thing, but now was the time to make it reliable, cost-effective, lightweight, compact, and efficient in all respects. In some ways, Jambor probably gave a sigh of relief when he surrendered his baby, as an incredible amount of time was required to convert a stunning idea into a stunning piece of engineering – even the boot width had to be looked at several times in order to accommodate the final mechanism.

Eventually, after a great deal of work, the entire mechanism – weighing just 33kg, or 73lb – was refined to give a luggage compartment space of 145 litres (5.1 cubic feet) when the top was retracted according to the VDA system, or 348 litres (12.3 cubic feet) when it was in the closed position. In countries where it was legal, one could opt for the run-flat tyre system, with a can of sealant and a compact electric pump taking the place of a cumbersome spare tyre, and this freed up another 21 litres (0.7 cubic feet) of space. To put this into perspective, the Mazda MX-5 from the same era was endowed with just 125 litres (4.4 cubic feet) of space, regardless of whether the hood was up or down. A clever touch was the addition of a pull-out cover to define the minimum storage space, and without this extended, the roof switch was isolated. This prevented damage to the roof and luggage being crushed at the same time.

Ultimately, in January 1996, Daimler-Benz got together with its Stuttgart neighbour Porsche to form Car Top Systems Fahrzeug-Dachsysteme GmbH in Hamburg. The CTS concern would serve both companies well in the development and manufacture of roof systems for their respective sports car models.

Actually, ASC in the States made something similar, releasing it a couple of years ahead of Mercedes on vehicles like the Mitsubishi 3000GT, although the cost of conversions limited sales. The 'Variodach' would bring the folding metal roof concept to a far wider, global audience, and at an affordable price, too – the ASC roof was the best part of $20,000, while the Benz marketing folks wanted to retail the SLK as a complete car with a $40,000 price-tag.

Autumn in Paris

A second SLK study vehicle put in an appearance at the 1994 Paris Salon, which ran from 6-16 October. This was a blue car that was similar to the Turin machine in most respects, but it came with the electro-hydraulically-operated 'Variodach' top and a more upmarket interior, decked out in contrasting shades of tan and blue suede.

A couple of views of the SLK concept car displayed at the 1994 Paris Salon, which opened its gates to the public on 6 October. The car had silver wheel centres when it appeared at the French event, and 'Étude SLK' on the registration plate to better suit its surroundings.

As it happens, careful inspection revealed a number of minor differences to augment the big changes. For instance, there was a different grille insert, colour-keyed wheels and door handles, a different exhaust layout, and exposed roll-over hoops with a folding wind-blocking screen installed behind them.

The fully-trimmed two-tone interior certainly looked appealing, but was never going to make it past the accounts department. It was endowed with an automatic transmission, switches for the power top, power mirrors and windows, and a stylized HVAC and audio control system, shaped to match the rearview mirror. Again, a lot of this was quite fanciful, but it was perhaps a lot closer to the interior of the production model in terms of equipment levels.

Peter Pfeiffer (Bruno Sacco's right-hand man at the time, and Chief Designer from the spring of 1999 following Sacco's retirement) said at the show: "This brings us another step closer to actually producing this model."

The timing was once more well-planned, for at the end of October, less than two weeks after the Paris Salon closed its doors for another couple of years, Mercedes-Benz presented its new Formula One car, launched in partnership with the British McLaren team. The partnership had to wait until March 1997 for its first win, but after that, it was easy to recall the domination of the 'Silver Arrows' of yore, not only in F1, but in the American CART (Indycar) series as well.

The final design

The Turin and Paris show cars had been excellent ambassadors and promotional tools for the SLK. They had a dream-like quality about them that inspired people, yet didn't stray too far away from the production model – a move that would have doubtless drawn strong criticism from all quarters had this been the case. The main differences came in the conversion of flashy details into something more practical, and the application of greater thought on the world's safety and lighting regulations. Production sequences and tooling had to be factored in, along with the assessment of materials that did the job required of them without giving the bean-counters a heart attack. There were also insurance matters to consider, with the cost and ease of panel replacement taken into account.

The front mask was already fairly close to the showroom design – at least in its basic features. However, for production, the grille was reduced in size and given a drilled honeycomb-style insert with a matt black finish that showed off the three-pointed star nicely. Above that was the Mercedes-Benz button badge that had appeared on the two show cars and generations

D
S LK 190

of SLs before them, but the headlight units were now oblong, rounded off on the inner edges and with clear indicator segments added on the outer edges, in-line with the bonnet shutline.

The bumper moulding was a little plain compared to the show cars – less aggressive, in reality. Where a swage line had been used to give the impression of a bumper blade before, a body-coloured insert was added on the production model in order to add a highlight on the flatter surface. On cars headed to the US, side markers were added to the ends of the inserts, which actually looked quite good – it was obviously not an afterthought. The number plate was kept at the same height, and the features below it were pretty much carried over, albeit simplified – the foglights remained in their original position, but the opening between them was now made up of heavy slats, and the lowest part of the air dam was painted black to visually reduce bulk.

As one glanced past the front-end, one could see the twin bulges in the bonnet had been retained, and the wipers still dropped into a recess below the trailing edge of the bonnet to improve aerodynamics, although the door mirrors had significantly grown in size – as expected given Mercedes' policy on safety. Nonetheless, the door mirror enclosures were shaped

Various views of the production car, this vehicle being used in a number of the earliest press releases, meaning it was actually a pre-production car. Mauer had said the SLK was designed to look its best with the top down, which is perhaps why so many of the press pictures show the car in open guise.

A pre-production model in the wind tunnel. Sporting an average Cd of 0.34, the aerodynamics were very sound on this car, reducing unwanted wind noise and enhancing fuel economy at the same time. Note the tiny splitters ahead of the front wheels, added to cut drag and reduce lift.

A one-fifth scale model in the water tunnel at Stuttgart University during the summer of 1996.

to cut through the air as part of the designer's war on drag, with work in the wind tunnel ultimately resulting in a very reasonable Cd figure of 0.33 (or 0.35 for grades with larger wheel and tyre combinations). Interestingly, a model of the SLK was also placed in the water tunnel at Stuttgart University. This novel style of testing became available too late in the R170 programme to make any changes, but it did at least back up the figures already collected using more traditional methods.

In profile, the nose was vaguely similar to the concept cars, apart from the way in which the various shapes and contours had been made, along with the indicator units, which now wrapped around the side to better serve their purpose. In addition, a repeater light was added to the trailing edge of the front wing (available for a number of uses depending on the car's destination), and supercharged vehicles carried a 'Kompressor' badge beneath this. The steep angle of the windscreen was retained, but the shutline below it was changed to give the car a more dynamic look – the door panel curved quite strongly rearward in the lower section, featuring similar matte black door handles to the Turin Show car.

The side sills were very plain, lacking the shapely lines of the show cars, but were blacked out anyway in a bid to make the production model look a touch more lithe regardless of the wheel and tyre combination specified (15-, 16- and 17-inch rims were available from the off). As per the show vehicles, the fuel filler lid was placed just aft of the door on the offside, which would be the passenger-side on a left-hand drive car. The rear wing profiles were actually very true to the machines displayed in Paris and Turin, with the wraparound bumper insert and blacked out section on the rear valance obvious changes, although careful inspection revealed a more rounded edge on the uppermost part of the tail, this being created by the combination light housing extending upwards.

Around the back, the red taillights were by far the clearest change, although they rose higher than they had in the show cars and became more triangular at the same time, aping those of the W202. The wraparound bumper inserts mentioned earlier ended roughly in line with the

The tasteful 'Kompressor' badge found on the front wings of the supercharged cars – the badging at the back gave no clue as to whether or not the vehicle was supercharged.

inner edges of the light clusters, and the lower edge of the valance was blacked out to trick the eye once more. The exhaust pipe was exposed underneath on the nearside, by the way, as per the Paris Show model (they had been hidden in the original Mauer design and a pair of exhausts had been used for the car shown in Turin). Other detail revisions included the addition of a lock on the right of the number plate, a third brakelight strip above the central Mercedes star, and a model designation badge in the upper left-hand corner of the boot lid.

Before moving on, we should mention that the roll-over hoops behind the seats were trimmed in a rather more serviceable padded vinyl, and the folding windblocker that had appeared in Paris was replaced by a plain panel that matched the hoops and looked a lot less fussy. Ultimately, a new wind-blocking screen was designed and marketed for the production cars – a simple net that dropped over the roll-over hoops and was clipped down to hold it in place.

The production version of the windblocking device – simple but effective. This angle also shows up the very subtle spoiler effect built into the bootlid – hardly ever visible, this tiny lip reduced drag by as much as one per cent.

DIMENSIONS

To help put the SLK's size into perspective, we have put together a table comparing the dimensions of the new car with the early 190SL (W121) and the R129 models, which represented the contemporary SL line at the time of the SLK's launch. The data on the Japanese interloper, credited with reviving the two-seat LWS (lightweight sports car) as a breed, provides a useful bench mark for reference, as does that for the Porsche Boxster – another open car that was making an impact, born in the same era as the SLK.

	SLK (R170)	190SL (W121)	500SL (R129)	Mazda MX-5	Porsche Boxster
Length	3995mm/157.3in	4220mm/166.1in	4470mm/176.0in	3970mm/156.3in	4315mm/169.9in
Wheelbase	2400mm/94.5in	2400mm/94.5in	2515mm/99.0in	2265mm/89.2in	2415mm/95.1in
Width	1715mm/67.5in	1740mm/68.5in	1812mm/71.3in	1675mm/65.9in	1780mm/70.1in
Front track	1488mm/58.6in	1430mm/56.3in	1535mm/60.4in	1405mm/55.3in	1455mm/57.3in
Reartrack	1485mm/58.5in	1475mm/58.1in	1523mm/60.0in	1420mm/55.9in	1508mm/59.4in
Height	1289mm/50.7in	1320mm/52.0in	1293mm/50.9in	1235mm/48.6in	1290mm/50.8in
Weight	1325kg/2915lb	1140kg/2508lb	1800kg/3960lb	940kg/2068lb	1250kg/2750lb

Note: The height entry is that for a hardtop (or when the top is in the raised position), while the width is for the body only, and does not include mirrors – these took the overall width to 1947mm (76.6in) in the case of the SLK. The rear track for the SLK is that with 16- or 17-inch wheels, which decreased by 15mm (0.6in) if 15-inch wheels were fitted. The weight is for the supercharged SLKs.

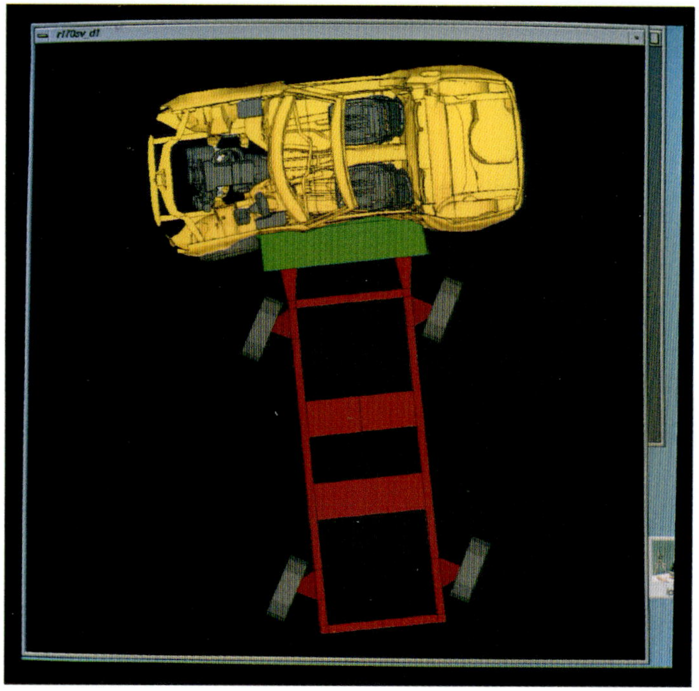

Safety

The Stuttgart brand had an enviable reputation for safety, established by the innovative ideas of Bela Barenyi and his team. Safety systems like crumple zones are taken for granted nowadays, but it was Barenyi that came up with the idea. Others chipped in with special door locks, advances in seatbelts and airbag technology and so on – you name it, the men and women in white coats at the Sindelfingen body plant had always been at the leading edge of advances in safety.

Open cars also had to uphold this legendary stature, earned the hard way during thousands of hours in the laboratory and testing facilities, which is easier said than done. The R107 SL had done a fine job of making convertibles safer in an overturning scenario, with its A-pillar being particularly strong. Thanks to a significant passage of time between

Computers were used to simulate various aspects of body strength, highlighting stress fractures, flexing and reactions to outside forces long before any prototypes were built. After a design had been selected, a small series of mock-ups was constructed, ultimately proving or disproving CAD theories.

A prototype shell being built up by hand. Many pre-production prototypes were required for all manner of testing, including a series of crash tests.

The production SLK's bodyshell, with high-tensile steel components painted in red in order to highlight them. Although aluminium panels were investigated for the bonnet, doors and bootlid, an all-steel body construction ultimately won the day on the grounds of cost control. However, the engineers won in a battle to offset the weight of the roof mechanism, with the rear firewall and roll-over hoop cover being made from a lightweight AZ91E magnesium alloy.

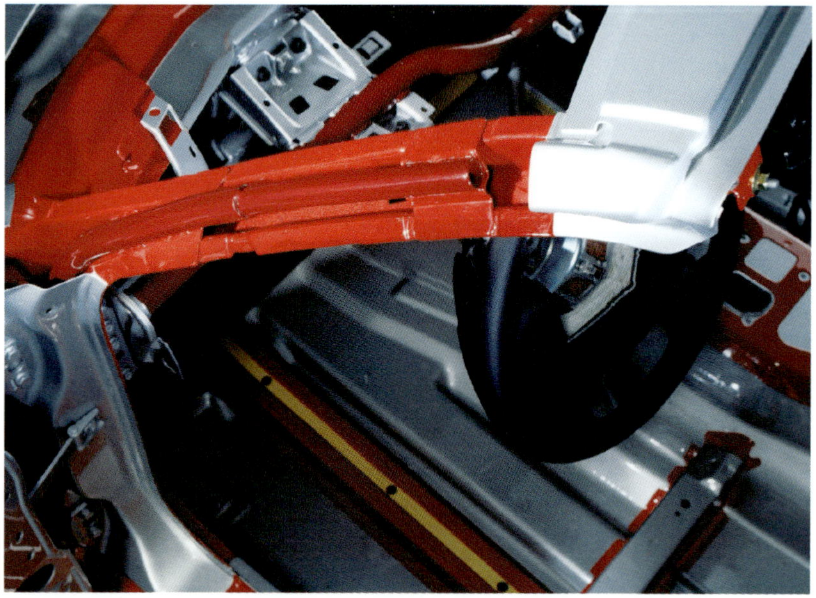

A close-up of the A-pillar with a tubular piece of steel added to enhance overall strength. Note also the tube running across the cockpit width at dashboard height which braced the two A-posts.

Detail shot of the roll-over hoop behind the seats. They may not have been the most attractive part of the design, but one can lay odds that more than a few people have appreciated their existence, some 20 years or so after the design was frozen.

A frontal collision staged in 1995. This type of offset crash test is not only a legal requirement in most countries, but the data collected is particularly useful for engineers, as the impact forces are concentrated on a smaller area. Any weakness in the car's body is exposed the split-second the vehicle hits the barrier.

generations, things were taken a stage further with the R129 version which replaced it, with a pop-up roll-over bar introduced into the equation. However, this added a lot of weight, complication and expense, which can be justified with ease on an expensive flagship, but not so readily on an entry-level convertible. So, for the R170 SLK, conventional and traditional methods of acquiring strength and safety had to be employed and duly refined …

When it comes to retaining torsional rigidity, converting a modern closed car into an open car often brings a number of problems, even if additional bracing pieces are added. At least being able to design the all-steel SLK as a monocoque convertible from the off eliminated this aspect, although the engineers still had to work hard to achieve a level of body rigidity which could rival that of a saloon – something one would expect from a Mercedes-Benz. It was not simply about getting rid of scuttle shake, as a strong body adds safety in many ways: the obvious one, giving the car its crashworthiness; a superior platform for suspension units to work properly and predictably, and improved comfort, which helps keep the driver focused on the job in hand. The SLK's unique roof, with its fine tolerances, was another reason for keeping body flex to an absolute minimum.

A roll-over test to prove the SLK was as safe as an open car possibly could be. Some tests were conducted with dummies; others, like this one, without.

Computer-aided design (CAD) and the very latest metal technology came to the rescue in keeping costs and weight down. The CAD programmes helped simulate the reactions of various design proposals when stress was applied to them, with shapes and metal types and thicknesses changed with ease until a design worthy of prototyping came to light. The CAD system could also be used to simulate accidents, allowing the engineering team to refine structures in order to control the rate of collapse in the body's crumple zones – the days of trial and error had disappeared long ago.

Special high-tensile steels were employed in crucial areas, such as the bulkheads surrounding the passenger compartment, and the rails that ran from just inside the front wheelwells and back to the rearmost corners of the cockpit. This expensive but lightweight option was adopted in other areas, too, including the

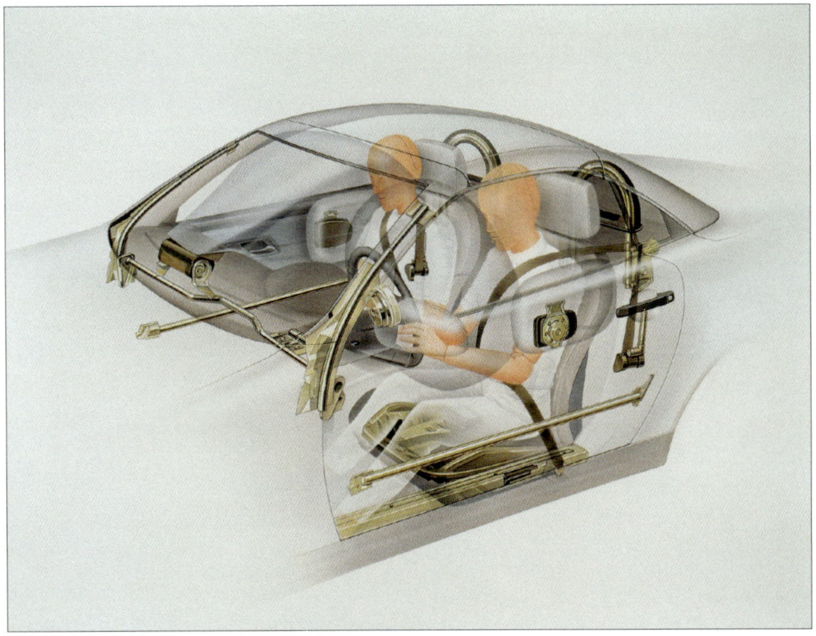

The passive safety systems of the R170 SLK's passenger compartment, with airbags in the steering wheel boss, ahead of the passenger in the upper part of the dashboard, and, as an option, in each door. Note also the side impact bars and seatbelt anchor points.

Detail shot of the optional side airbags, which also serves as a useful reference for the door furniture.

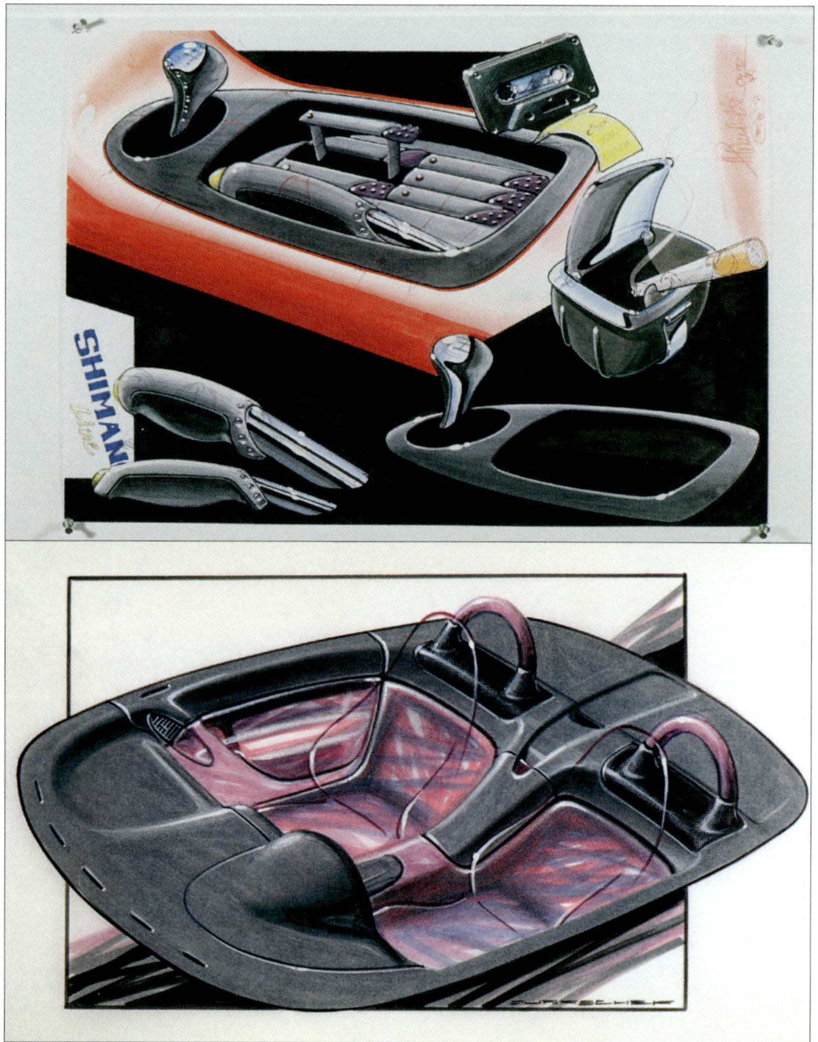

A couple of the more futuristic interior designs put forward in the early stages of reviving the R170 project.

bumper hangers, the crossmember holding up the front of the engine, the sills, and transmission tunnel bracing. In addition, for extra shell strength, round-section tubing was added to the inside of the A-pillars, underneath the dashboard (mounted just above the steering column), in the doors, and behind the seats – the latter being the exposed hoops that would take the weight of the car in a roll-over situation, giving passengers valuable survival space in a bad crash if the top was down. With the top up, the 'Variodach' was designed with a sturdy frame on the outer edges in another bid to protect occupants if the car

Hans-Peter Wunderlich working on an interior design sketch. Most of the drawings on the board were done during 1992 and 1993.

turned over. Research in Germany had shown that an open car was more likely to be involved in a roll than a side impact, so this R&D work was deemed to be of particular importance.

Augmenting the passive safety package were dual front airbags, side airbags, and seatbelt tensioners and force limiters, all adding up to give the SLK levels of safety comparable with a luxury saloon.

The SLK's interior

It should be borne in mind that the SLK concept was quite unlike that of the average Benz of the 1970s or 1980s, in order to appeal to a new sector of the market. The older, more conservative cars had a strong following, the author included amongst the fans of the marque's products from the time, but 'fun' was hardly a word that could be readily applied to them. To get new faces into the showroom, a fresh, lighter approach was required, and, to a far greater extent than the exterior styling, it was via the interior that the designers found a way in which the SLK could distance itself from the SL and reach out to a younger audience.

The interior of the 1994 Turin Show car had been deliberately excessive, as it was a sure way of filling column inches in the motoring press. However, if one looks at the basic structures and layout, it wasn't that far from the production model – a touch hopeful rather than pure fantasy. In much the same way, the Paris Show car was built to be memorable, but it provided

This 1992 sketch was actually very close to the production design, with a T-shaped dashboard and integrated centre console running the length of the transmission tunnel. The steering wheel, the three separate instruments under a simple top roll, the HVAC controls, and the two-tone colouring were all remarkably similar to the final design.

stronger hints still as to what was to come in 1996, with the instrument backs now covered by a sprawling top roll. Imagine simpler shapes to ease manufacturing, less ornate controls and instruments, and a more realistic choice of trim materials – all things that one has come to expect in the transformation of show car to production car – and we're already getting fairly close to the real thing.

If one looks at a domestic production car (lhd), starting with the dashboard, the top roll featured a pair of vents for the screen, and smaller defroster vents for clearing the side windows at each extremity. There was an airbag section for the passenger side, and a pull-out tray in the centre, usually for sunglasses or suchlike, although a cupholder/coin box insert could be specified. It arched upwards in a semi-circle in front of the driver, matching the shape of the instrument housing.

Below the black-coloured top roll, it's almost possible to separate things into three modules: the one in front of the driver contained an air vent, master light switch and beam height adjuster to the left of the steering column; the bank of analogue

With the basic shapes in place, another team of designers worked on material selection and colouring, giving the car a light, friendly atmosphere that still appeared classy – a remarkably difficult balance to strike.

This manual car (left) with black leather trim shows the overall layout of the interior. The production cars had a coloured Mercedes-Benz badge in the centre of the steering wheel pad, which helped brighten up things no end. The cloth version of the black trim (right), again in pre-production form. This car has an automatic transmission and a full bank of switches beneath the radio. From left to right, these are for seat heating control; headlamp washers; the ASR on/off switch; hazard warning lights; a central locking trip switch; alarm indicator, and a heated seat switch for the passenger. Note the chrome gate surround and selector layout on the automatic gearbox.

instruments and warning lights above it, and the ignition barrel to the right of it. The bonnet release was in the lower left-hand corner, pretty much out of sight, although the drilled pedal set was something quite different – designed to be seen.

The meter pack was made up of a central 260kph speedometer with a digital trip and main odometer in the lower section, and warning lights for the indicators and hazard lights. The tachometer was slightly smaller and positioned to the right of the speedo, with a digital clock in the lower part of it (adjusted by a spindle to the left); the matching meter to the left of the speedo contained gauges for coolant temperature and fuel level, along with a digital outside temperature readout. All three meters had light ivory-coloured gauge faces with dark grey calibrations, red pointers and chrome outer bezels – the black hooded effect used to stop stray reflections on them. There was a rheostat to the right of the outside temperature gauge, and a selection of warning lights grouped together in both the left- and right-hand corners of the instrument binnacle. Interestingly, when the lights were on, the meter faces became grey with red calibrations, and digital read-outs became black on red.

The chunky 380mm (15in) diameter, four-spoke steering wheel was trimmed in black leather, with the upper spokes serving as horn pushes. Like the door inserts, centre console moulding and seat inserts, these pieces matched the colour of the dashboard fascia, which was either charcoal grey or a contrasting shade of red, green, dark blue or a light beige. The black centre boss containing the SRS airbag was plain on early press pictures, but the embossed three-pointed star was changed for a proper coloured roundel in time for production. Telescopic adjustment was available on the steering column, but the bracing bar running along the front of the cockpit ruled out a tilt facility. Beyond the wheel was the indicator stalk with high beam and

windscreen wash/wipe controls, and a cruise control stalk above that, if fitted.

Moving to the central section, it extended from the sunglasses/cupholder tray in the top roll all the way back to the bulkhead behind the seats, the panel being carpeted in the same material as the footwells. Cut into a faux carbon trim piece that continued downwards to create a gearlever surround, air vents were placed directly beneath the tray, with the HVAC controls below them, including a pair of thumbwheels (as had become a tradition at Mercedes) for separate temperature control on either side of the cockpit. Moving down again, the radio slot came next, followed by a bank of switches that varied from car to car, depending on the options fitted – the only guaranteed constant was the red triangular button in the centre for the hazard warning lights. At the base was a small, open storage box and an ashtray, before the angle of the carbon-style trim changed to follow the profile of the transmission tunnel. The central gearlever was

The instrument pack in daylight, with two banks of warning lights to the outer edges …

… and the same gauges once the lights were switched on. This is the instrument pack for a domestic model, with its speedometer calibrated to 260kph. The red-line also indicates a 2-litre car, as the 2.3-litre models were red-lined at 5800rpm.

This close-up gives a good view of the side air vents, master lighting switch, indicator stalk, pedal set (automatic cars also had drilled pedals), and the standard treadplate design.

A close-up of the centre stack, giving a clear view of the heating and ventilation controls.

surrounded on both sides by rocker switches for the electric windows, and a small button off to the right, close to the storage box to enable the passenger-side airbag to be disabled in case a child seat was being used. Doing away with a foot-operated parking brake, the handbrake was aft of the gearlever, and to its right was a power mirror adjuster and a red roof-shaped button that looked after the power top. There was a covered oddments box in the same plane as the switches, with a cigarette lighter contained within, and a larger storage box aft of that with a hinged lid.

The third section, above the passenger's legs, contained a large, lockable glovebox, and an air vent off to the far right, which, like the vent and lighting switches on the other side, was mounted on a carbon-style ('Carbon Optic') plinth. Looking up to the top rail, there were folding sunvisors, an interior light with its own dedicated switch, and an oval-shaped rearview mirror with a manual dipping feature.

The power mirror toggle switch and the red roof-shaped one that operated the power top. The chrome ledge allowed the owner to open or close the narrow storage box that sat alongside the handbrake.

The handbrake, small storage box (open in this shot to reveal the cigarette lighter), and the main centre cubby in detail. The latter could be fitted with a number of inserts to best suit the car's audio configuration.

A useful shot in many ways, as it shows off the glovebox, door trim and treadplates nicely. A switch was provided close to the gearlever to switch off the passenger-side airbag whenever a childseat was fitted, otherwise the force of the bag opening would probably do more damage to a youngster than a light accident. Nonetheless, this was still a novel feature at the time. The badge in the centre of the road wheel is similar to that fitted to the steering wheel pad on production cars, by the way. Note also the fuel filler lid – the locking and release of this panel was ultimately linked to the car's central locking system.

The door trim panels were kept simple, with a black capping to match the dashboard's top roll that ultimately created a frame for a coloured insert that matched the fascia. The door pull and armrest were integrated into this insert, with the chrome door release handle set in an attractive chrome housing at the leading edge of the door pull, trimmed with a carbon-style plinth; it also featured a twitter speaker unit. Below the armrests were soft map pockets, with the main door speaker units ahead of these. The standard treadplates were black plastic with stainless steel inserts.

The bucket seats were seriously sporty by Mercedes standards, with upturned sides on the lower cushion and heavy

The structure of the bucket seats, made by Recaro of Stuttgart, and featuring lightweight magnesium alloy in the frame.

A final view of the interior, this one trimmed in the attractive black and red two-tone leather combination. Again, please ignore the steering wheel centre pad, but otherwise, the image is true to production status. Note the contrasting stitching on the upholstery, and also the soft pouch in the centre of the bulkhead, used to store the windblocker.

side bolsters on the backrest. The outer section of the upholstery was black, along with the adjustable headrests, and the inserts were trimmed to match the dashboard fascia, centre console and door trim inserts. The contrasting stitching and moulded backing shell, coloured to suit to the trim's hue, added to the sporting impression. Fore and aft adjustment was via a long lever at the front of the seat; movement of the lower cushion was via a lever on the outer edge of the base, and the backrest angle was looked after by a hefty knob positioned above the seatbelt receiver. Map nets could be added behind the seats, and the windblocker screen was carried in a soft pouch in the centre of the rear bulkhead.

Surprisingly for such a small car, even compared to the larger SL, the interior felt quite light and roomy. This was largely due to a change in design eras, when airbags – increasingly compact versions, at that – could replace softer, heavily-cushioned surfaces in the name of safety. Add in modern seatbelt technology (which reduced the need for elaborate padding), along with a desire to equip the car with only the essentials for driving and slim seats, and it's easy to see where the extra space was gained. This would be another feather in the cap for the marketing men to work with, for some of the smaller roadsters were actually quite claustrophobic, especially for taller drivers, and in Europe and America, there's plenty of those.

Continued on page 71

TESTING, TESTING ...

The SLK went through an exhaustive testing programme, both in the hallowed halls of Stuttgart and in tens of thousands of road miles in all corners of the globe – sometimes calling upon engineers to flaunt their skills along the way. But the result of all this hard work, encompassing everything from measuring the flow of air through the cockpit and wear and tear on individual components, to driving in extremes of heat, cold, humidity and dust, ultimately gave buyers a reliable machine worthy of carrying the three-pointed star on its nose.

A round-the-world trip with the SLK prototypes, from scorching dustbowls to frozen wastes, and everything in between ...

NU AR 78

NU YF 72

RAILROAD
CROSSING
2
TRACKS
STOP
117
110

An engine and transmission being tortured on a test rig, with the exhaust pipes glowing red from the heat build-up.

One of the early test track hacks being deluged with water to ensure that all of the car's seals could withstand the very worst of rainstorms.

An SLK prototype receiving a frosty reception.

Another prototype on a Schenck shaking rig, simulating years of hard use in a relatively short space of time. These tests ran day and night, and quickly highlighted reliability problems in chassis components, and potential weaknesses in the body structure.

Testing for the effects of backdraft through the cockpit when a car is driven at speed allowed the engineers to refine the windblocker design.

Dieter Zetsche (by the driver's-side door) checking over the final windblocker design with engineers. A contemporary R129 SL (closest to the camera) and the convertible version of the W124 are on hand for comparison.

The 2-litre NA version of the M111 engine installed in the SLK.

Drivetrain

The SLK was launched with three straight-four M111 engine variations – a pair of 2-litre units (one normally-aspirated and one with forced induction), and a supercharged 2.3-litre unit. The smaller supercharged lump was released to a very limited number of markets where taxes were extremely high on cars with engine capacities above a 2-litre threshold.

The water-cooled M111 engine series can be traced back to the W124 saloons, with the 2-litre normally-aspirated unit appearing in time for the 1993 season. Numerous variations followed, with most of them gaining variable intake camshaft timing in August 1996 – a clever electromagnetically-controlled hydraulic device that simply took the place of the regular chain sprocket. At idle, there was zero overlap, but the inlet valves were made to stay open longer under acceleration or at higher revs, thus enhancing the power-unit's overall efficiency.

In the case of the 2-litre NA lump, the compression ratio was increased from 9.6 to 10.4:1 at the same time, and the Type 111.941 engine code was changed to a 111.945 one. Developing 136bhp, it was hardly a ball of fire, but it was clean and reliable. After inheriting the new camshaft arrangement, power increased from 180 to 192bhp on the supercharged version (Type 111.944), although the c/r and engine code were unchanged. It was a similar story with the 2.3-litre supercharged variant (Type 111.975), which developed 193bhp. These engines were later shared with the CLK, another two-door machine that made use of the C-Class structure and parts bin, but the SLK versions were given their own model-specific code numbers.

The basic M111 structure was made up of a cast iron block and an aluminium alloy head, mounted in the car in a conventional, longitudinal manner to suit a rear-wheel drive configuration. The iron block may have been heavier than an alloy one, but it was better at damping noise, and an awful lot cheaper to produce. With engineers trying to keep the sales price down to a point where the SL and SLK were in completely different market sectors, the latter was an important factor, and won out above the desire to meet a target weight. Casting a new component would have cost a fortune, and in any case, using a block that had already been proved in service gave huge benefits that were hard to deny. Interestingly, the oil sump was an alloy casting.

The forged steel crankshaft ran in five main bearings, with drive taken to the camshafts at the top-end by a duplex chain tensioned by a pair of slippers. The dohc head contained four valves per cylinder, with a pair of inlets per pot operated by a dedicated camshaft on the induction side, and a pair of exhaust valves with their own camshaft opposite them. The camshaft lobes acted on bucket tappets with hydraulic clearance adjustment, with each valve below angled inwards towards the single central sparkplug. Fuel-injection was the norm, with the intake manifold and plenum chamber as a single-piece alloy casting, but the control systems varied between engine types, and there were also normally-aspirated and forced-induction variants.

On the opposite side of the head, the fabricated exhaust manifold was made up of a compact four-into-two section that merged two downpipes to give a single exit into the catalytic converter section, and then a hefty rear silencer on the way back to the tailpipe. US-spec models had a different 'cat' to European and Japanese models, while the NA cars employed a unique catalytic converter and also added a centre box into the equation.

As far as the SLK was concerned, the base car came with the 2-litre NA Type 111.946 unit. The alloy pistons, attached to conventional split connecting rods, had short skirts and three rings, running within a 89.9mm (3.5in) bore and 78.7mm (3.1in) stroke measurement to give a cubic capacity of 1998cc. The indirect fuel-injection was controlled by the VDO MSE management system with a hot film air mass sensor, while a pair of coils looked after the four sparkplugs until the face-lift in 2000.

Ancillaries, such as the viscous-coupled cooling fan, water pump, alternator, PAS pump and air-conditioning pump, ran off a ribbed belt, but the oil pump employed a single-row chain off the nose of the crank for its drive. It's also worth noting at this point that cars with air-conditioning had an electric cooling fan.

Sporting a 10.4:1 compression ratio, the 111.946 engine (or M111 E20) developed 136bhp at 5500rpm, and 140lbft of torque at between 3700 and 4500rpm. It could be linked to a Getrag GL68/20H-5 five-speed manual gearbox (code 717.417), coming with internal ratios of 3.91, 2.17, 1.37, 1.00 and 0.81 combined with a 3.91:1 final-drive, although the J-5 version (717.418), albeit with all the same ratios, was used for cars without a dual-mass flywheel – best summed up as those without air-conditioning. The other option was a Daimler

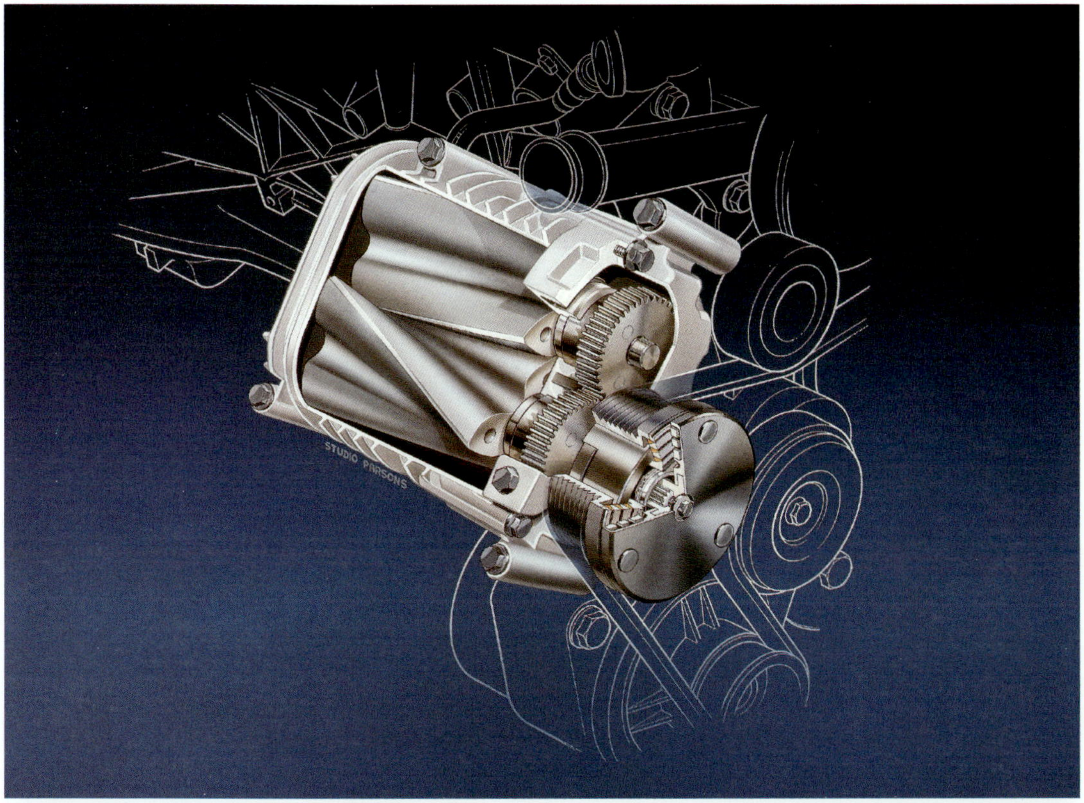

Opposite page: An early version of the supercharged engine used in the SLK (production versions destined for the two-seater had a red sparkplug cover to dress the top of the unit, as well as an electric cooling fan whenever air-conditioning was fitted), plus a closeup of the Eaton supercharger (left). The supercharger revived the romance of the prewar era, although this latest version, with its three-lobe rotors, was quieter and far more efficient.

Engine bay of the SLK230 Kompressor model.

AG-built, electronically-controlled five-speed automatic known as the 5G-Tronic in Mercedes speak, or the NAG1 within the Chrysler organization. This particular 5AT was the W5A330 unit (722.602), with a lock-up torque converter and fuzzy logic software to adapt to driver styles. It came listed with 3.93 on first, 2.41 on second, 1.49 on third, a direct fourth, and an overdriven 0.83 on fifth. The final-drive ratio was the same as that specified for the manual car: 3.91:1.

The Type 111.943 supercharged 2-litre engine (or M111 E20 ML) was produced for the Italian, Greek and Portuguese markets. Apart from the Bosch Motronic engine management system, and all the plumbing for the supercharger (including an intercooler), it was much the same as the NA unit. With an 8.5:1 c/r, it developed a healthy 192bhp at 5300rpm, and 199lbft of torque within a useful 2500 to 4800rpm rev-range. There was no automatic option available with this car – the Getrag GL76/29A-5 five-speed manual (717.460) was the only transmission available, with 3.86 on first, 2.18 on second, 1.38 on third, 1.00 on fourth, and 0.80 on fifth; final-drive was listed at 3.46:1.

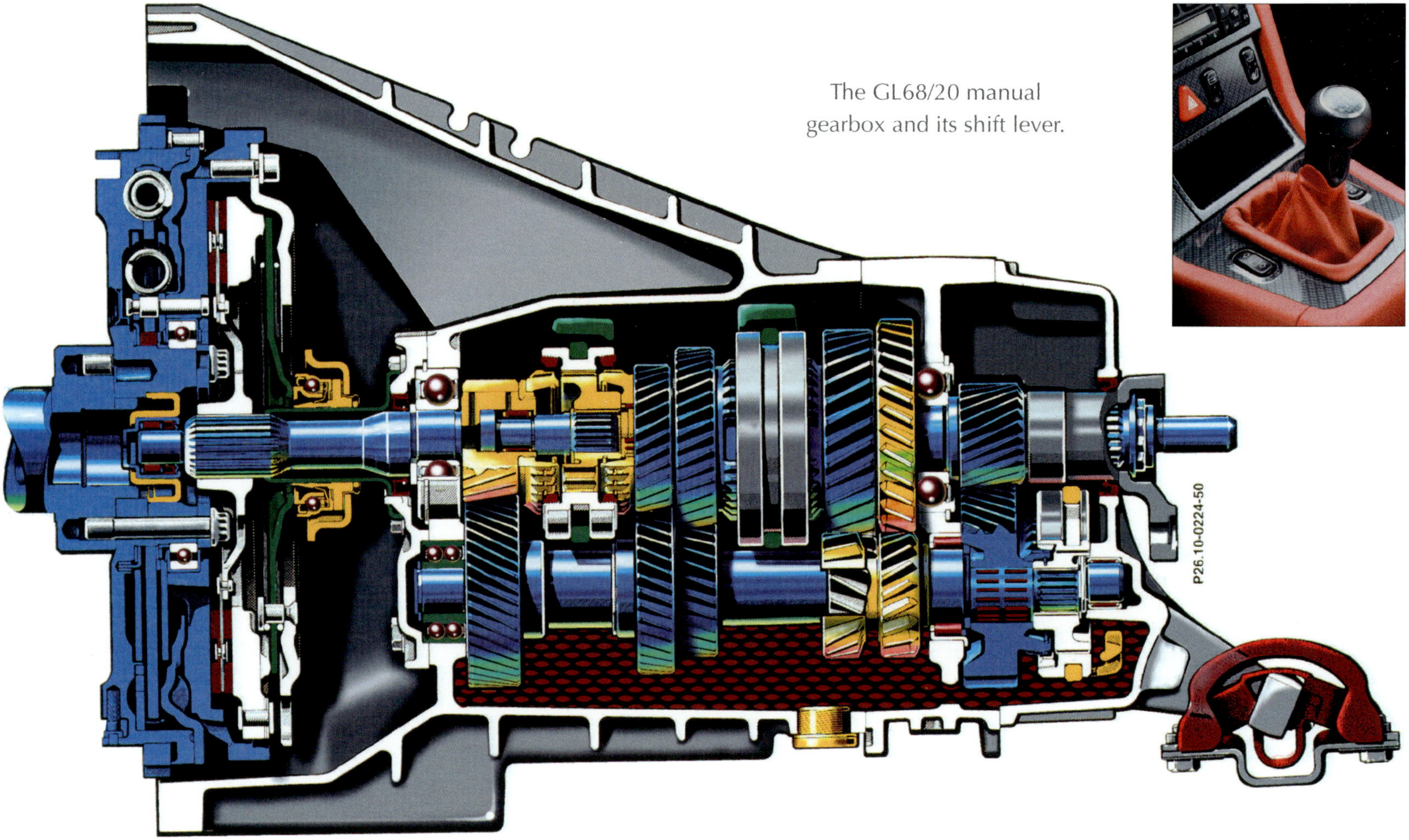

The GL68/20 manual gearbox and its shift lever.

5-Gang-Schaltgetriebe GL68/20

The Type 111.973 (M111 E23 ML) engine was used in the early SLK230 'Kompressor' models. This was similar to the 2-litre supercharged unit, with its Eaton M62 blower and intercooler arrangement, Bosch ME 2.1 management system and hot film air mass sensor, although the bore was enlarged slightly to 90.9mm, while the stroke was much longer, listed at 88.4mm. With an 8.8:1 compression ratio, the 2295cc unit pumped out 193bhp at 5300rpm, and 207lbft of torque between 2500 and 4800rpm. Due to different exhaust systems, the 2.3-litre variant was given a '19N' code for the US, '19K' for Canada, and '19L' for Japan, although power and torque outputs were the same for all markets.

The manual transmission, available in Europe and North America only (Japan and Australia were restricted to the 5AT version), was the same as that specified in the 2-litre supercharged car, carrying the same type and code numbers, as well as the internal ratios and 3.46:1 final-drive. As for the automatic transmission, this was the same W5A330 unit as that employed for the strict (as in normally-aspirated) SLK200, with the same 3.93, 2.41, 1.49, 1.00 and 0.83 cogs, too, although a taller 3.27:1 final-drive ratio was specified to better suit the engine's characteristics. This particular version of the W5A gearbox carried the 722.605 code.

Manual gearboxes had four shift planes, with reverse to the left and down, first through fourth in a central 'H', and fifth up and to the right. The automatics had their traditional staggered gate pattern, and came with an S/W switch for swapping to a

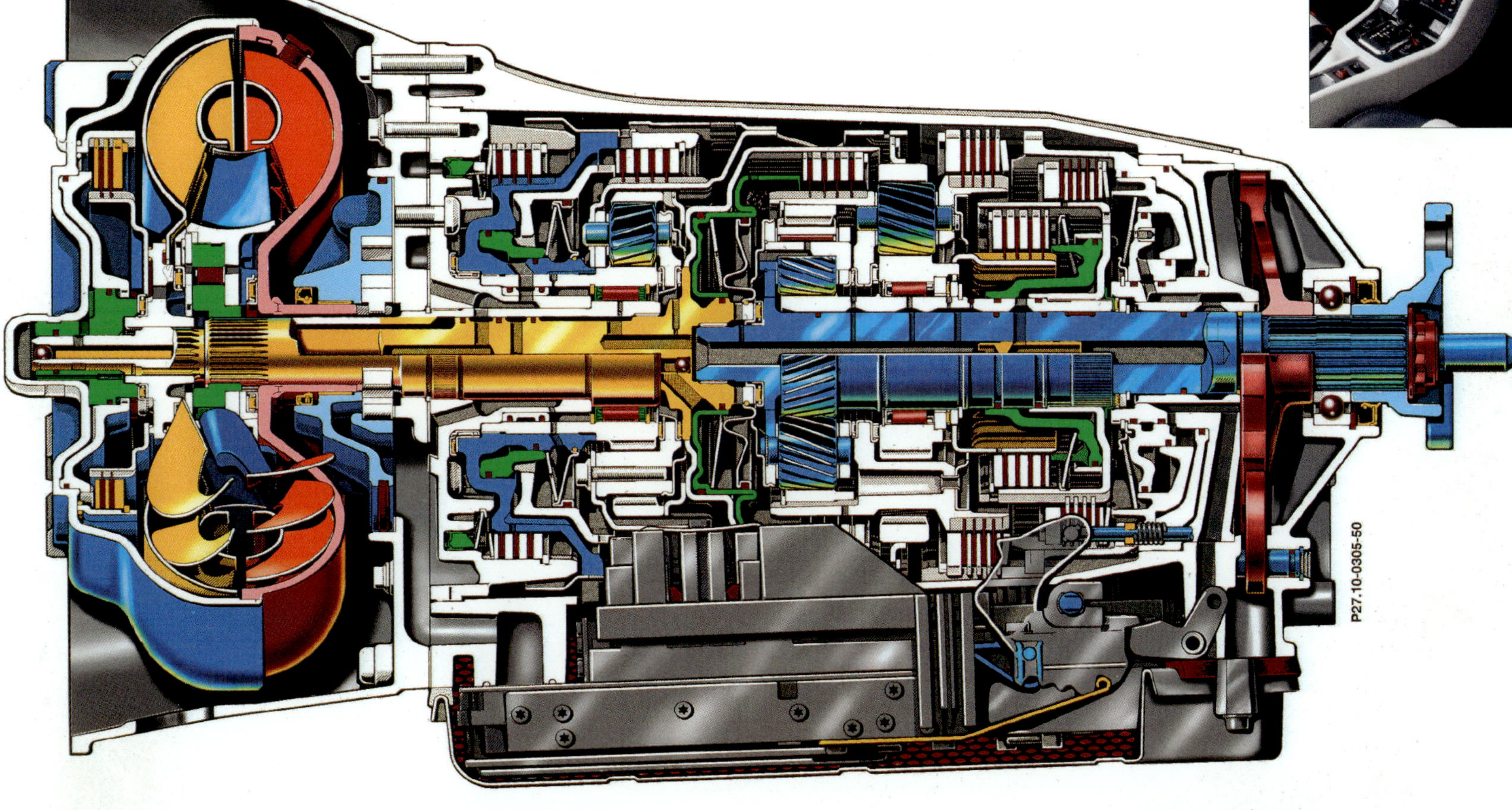

The W5A330 automatic transmission and the interior of an automatic car with the light-beige (quartz) trim – this was the lightest shade available, and in many ways, works the best with the carbon-style inserts. The so-called '5G-Tronic' gearbox had been announced in early 1995, and was first used in the new S600 Coupé launched that May before filtering through to other model lines.

winter (or wet) driving mode. This allowed the car to start in second gear instead of first, unless manually selected or in a kickdown situation, and executed upshifts lower down the rev-range to improve traction. Cruise control was available on the automatic cars.

It was all very conventional at the back, with the two-piece propshaft running to a cast iron axle housing, from which the driveshafts sprouted. These were bolted in place to the differential unit, with a CV joint and splined section at the wheel end that ran within a hub carrier and connected to the wheel flange.

Chassis components

The chassis setup was based on contemporary C-Class practice, but with spring and damper rates, as well as the wheel travel, suitably tuned and adjusted to be more in-keeping with a sports car. From the start, the assumption was made that buyers would be more interested in superior handling dynamics than a small sacrifice in low-speed ride quality.

At the front, there was a broad-based lower wishbone carrying the inboard coil spring, and also providing a connection for the gas-filled telescopic shock absorber close to the wheel. A trackrod end then attached the lengthy steering knuckle and hub

Drawing of the front suspension and braking system of the R170, along with the steering system. The long wheel travel of the C-Class donor car was retained for comfort, but subtle tuning of the spring and damper rates stiffened things a touch.

carrier, which was located at the top by a very narrow control arm, or a second wishbone if you want to call it that. The anti-roll bar ran in front of the suspension, with the steering mechanism aft of it.

The multi-link rear suspension was based on a hefty cradle that connected to the body with rubber bushes at four points. A short control arm carried the inboard coil spring and the outboard damper, and the other four arms (giving five links in all) then secured and located the hub carrier.

Not surprisingly, given the track record of the Stuttgart engineers, the tried and tested recirculating ball power-assisted steering system was called up for duty once more, with a damper in the linkage to take out road shocks transmitted to the steering wheel. With a ratio of 15.5:1 (a 12 per cent quicker setup than that of the C-Class saloons), it took just over three turns of the wheel to go from lock to lock.

The servo-assisted, dual-circuit brake system came with ABS (anti-lock braking system) as standard. A 288mm (11.3in)

The rear suspension and brakes, as well as the cradle that carried the module. The differential unit and driveshafts are also visible.

The standard 15-inch alloy wheel used on NA cars, left, and the standard 16-inch wheels employed by supercharged cars.

diameter ventilated disc was used up front with a floating calliper on the leading edge, while a solid 278mm (10.9in) disc was specified for the rear, complete with a fixed calliper on the trailing edge and an integral drum so that shoes could be used for the handbrake mechanism. Drums always give a far more efficient parking brake, while discs are better at pulling a car down from speed, so this was an ideal compromise.

Supercharged cars came with ASR (standing for Antriebsschlupfregelung), while the normally-aspirated model was available with ETS – a very basic, low-speed electronic traction control system that wasn't able to govern engine power. ASR, on the other hand, was a state-of-the-art traction control system, managing the rear brake activation and power sent to the rear wheels as soon as slippage was detected in order to give the best possible traction in all conditions. The ASR setup also monitored cornering speeds and road curvature via four ABS sensors on the rear axle, and automatically reduced engine revs if there was a high potential for loss of control. Incidentally, ASR disengaged as soon as the brakes were applied, and there was also a switch to fine-tune the system to better suit the use of snow chains. However, it could not be switched off. Eventually, both cars were given the ASR system, but that's something we'll come to later on in the book.

The car's aluminium alloy wheels were attached to the vehicle by five bolts. The normally-aspirated model came with 7J x 15 seven-spoke rims shod with 205/60 HR-rated rubber at both ends, although the sculptured cut-outs made them look like a traditional steel disc wheel – part of the plan no doubt to give the car a retro aura. Supercharged cars had regular seven-spoke alloys, but with 16-inch diameter rims, and different widths front to rear – 7J with 205/55 VR-rated tyres up front, and 8J combined with 225/50s at the back. Some (but certainly not all) supercharged cars, had a small rubber lip added to the rear wheelarch. It was actually listed as a standard feature on home market 'Kompressor' cars, but seems a very hit and miss item, and is hardly ever seen on export models.

Cutaway drawing of the R170 SLK showing the location of all the main components. About the only thing not possible to see with ease is the 53-litre (11.6 Imperial, or 14.0 US gallon) fuel tank, which was located behind the seats.

In the background

Jürgen Schrempp was named as the new Chairman of the Board of Management at Daimler-Benz AG in May 1995, a month before the launch of the twin-headlight W210 E-Class saloon. The fresh front mask design had first been revealed in a concept car displayed at the 1993 Geneva Show, and it became something of a Benz signature for a little while.

At the 1995 Frankfurt Show, held in September, the crowds were treated to a series of upgrades for the SL and C-Class, as well as the launch of the E50 AMG saloon. The AMG name was flying high in both the DTM and ITC touring car racing series' at this time, the competition programme being treated as a partnership between the Stuttgart and Affalterbach companies. As it happens, AMG had secured a deal in which its tuning parts could be sold and fitted via Mercedes-Benz dealerships in October 1990, and complete cars started filtering through into domestic showrooms by May 1991. The two concerns would become closer still in the future, with Mercedes taking a 51 per cent stake in the firm in January 1999, but their relationship, even at this stage, brought forth a range of officially approved tuning parts to allow owners greater individuality, and the success on the tracks was a magnificent marketing tool for all concerned.

On the subject of individuality, the first Designo consulting centre opened at the Sindelfingen plant in November 1995. This allowed customers to order cars with special interior and exterior finishes, adding to the enjoyment of purchasing a new car and the years of ownership ahead. Five more centres were planned for Germany, although the Designo name would eventually hold worldwide appeal.

While the 1996 Geneva Show was used to launch a new line of C- and E-Class estates, the 66th Turin Show, held in the following month, was reserved to give the R170 SLK a full share of the limelight. The scene was set for another date in Turin ...

The face-lifted version of the R129 SL, announced in September 1995.

The real movers in the SLK project were Dieter Zetsche (left, aka Dr Z) and Jürgen Hubbert, seen here on the right, and responsible for passenger car development. Zetsche was Hubbert's boss at the time of the SLK project, but when Hubbert was promoted to executive status in 1995, Helmut Petri (centre) moved up to take his place. At last, the car was ready to greet the world ...

3

THE PRODUCTION MODELS

"The Mercedes-Benz SLK, the long-awaited 'baby SL' that goes on sale here early next year, may be a hit even before one of these retractable hardtop sports cars is sold. The German automaker says it has firm orders for 25,000 of them around the world ..." – *Car & Driver*, July 1996.

For many in the hallowed halls of Stuttgart the hard work had ended, while for others it was just about to begin. After years of development, the SLK was finally ready for production, and with engineering teams moving on to the next project, it was the turn of the sales and marketing folks to do their magic, as well as those handling the less glamorous though equally important work of preparing the owner and workshop manuals, and briefing dealers and mechanics on the new car. It was also time to set the production lines in motion – the ultimate acid test for months of preparation and planning, and the dependability of component supply routes. This was the part that enthusiasts took for granted – they were more interested in what the car looked and drove like. While most still had to wait a little longer to drive the SLK, the opportunity to at least see the production model at last presented itself in Italy during the spring of 1996.

Another date in Turin

At 9:30am on Monday 22 April, the press started streaming through the gates at the 1996 Turin Show. This was the 66th time the Salone dell'automobile di Torino had been held: traditionally a showcase for the Italian coachbuilders to display their flair, and even in the modern era, there was still an element of anticipation as enthusiasts pondered on what the likes of Pininfarina and Bertone would be creating for the event.

Once the press and dignitaries had cleared away, the show opened to the public on 25 April, running until 5 May. That year, visitors were treated to a fine selection of concept cars, from the Bertone Enduro to the ItalDesign Legram: the IDEA Vuscia; the Giannini Windsurf; the Pininfarina Eta Beta; the Zagato Bravo Bis; the Maggiora Barchetta Coupé; the Ghia Saetta, and the Stola Dedica. But the biggest news by far was the world premiere of the production version of the R170 SLK ...

It will be remembered that the Italian event had played host to the first prototype's debut two years earlier, so it was only fitting that Mercedes-Benz chose Turin to unveil the showroom version of the two-seater, with F1 pilot Mika Hakkinen putting in a guest appearance for good measure. As it happens, everyone had a very good idea of what the car would look like, for the company had already leaked official pictures of the SLK as early as October 1995, with a silver-coloured machine (registration S-LK 9608) acting a multi-role part as both a normally-aspirated and a supercharged car for photography purposes.

Thinking about it, with heat from the competition getting stronger by the day, it certainly wasn't a bad idea to keep the SLK in press focus. Having got the bean-counters happy with the figures at last, with European sales of open cars rising from 11,300 units in 1992 to 98,500 in 1995, there was always the worry that the market would become saturated before the Benz had a chance to hit the dealerships. The maths had been calculated on

Continued on page 92

The catalogue illustrated over the following pages was produced in readiness of the 1996 Turin Show, its zestful and stylish images confirming that the SLK was aimed at winning over a younger audience. It was thought that the attractive pricing and less serious styling would appeal to those who had never previously bought a Mercedes-Benz. From the buzz created by the new model in the local classic car meetings I was attending at the time of the launch, it seemed like a fair assumption.

SLK – die 3 Buchstaben am Heck unseres neuen Roadsters stehen für sportlich, leicht, kurz. Damit heißt das Auto genauso, wie es fährt: sportlich, leichtfüßig und extrem wendig – ein konsequenter Sportwagen in bester Mercedes-Benz Qualität und Tradition: Motor vorn, Antrieb hinten und dazwischen jede Menge Spaß. Dabei hat man die Wahl zwischen dem 2-Liter-Motor und der 2,3-Liter-Kompressormaschine, die den Spaßfaktor noch mal erhöht.
S LP 7685

Der Urahn des SLK erblickte 1954 in New York die Blitzlichter dieser Welt. Allerdings ging der 190 SL erst im Mai 1955 in Serie. Als erschwinglicher Zweisitzer mit 4-Zylinder-Motor entwickelte er sich sofort zum Verkaufsschlager. Obwohl mehr zum Flanieren als zum Imponieren gedacht, machte der 190 SL auch auf den Rennstrecken Eindruck. Beim Grand Prix von Macao 1956 sah man den flotten Roadster sogar als Sieger über die Ziellinie flitzen.
Weltpremiere 1954 in New York: 190 SL und 300 SL.
Am 8. Februar 1963 lief der 25.881. und damit auch der letzte Mercedes 190 SL vom Band. Mittlerweile ist der kleine Roadster ein echtes Liebhaberstück geworden, das von seinen Besitzern nur noch bei Sonnenschein aus der Garage geholt wird.
Er sollte nie ein Rennwagen sein: Trotzdem gewann der 190 SL in Macao, holte sich die Siegeslorbeeren 1956 beim Grand Prix von Casablanca in der GT-Klasse und wurde Klassensieger bei der Hong Kong Rallye 1958.
BOSCH
Auch ein enger Verwandter des SLK: der Deutsche Tourenwagen-Meister 94/95.
S LL 1611
S LP 7685

Lange Motorhaube, langer Radstand, kurzes Heck – ein Blick auf die Karosserie des SLK verrät sofort das Design-Konzept: pure Sportlichkeit. Die ausgeprägte Keilform und die fließenden Übergänge der Karosserie verleihen dem Auto zusätzlich Dynamik und Eleganz. Wie bei unseren legendären Roadstern wölben sich auf der Motorhaube zwei sogenannte „Power Domes".
für die
d ent-
ießlich
sehen.

Mercedes-Benz hat sich nie damit zufriedengegeben, einfach nur gute Autos zu bauen. Jedes neue Modell, das wir in den letzten 100 Jahren auf die Straße gebracht haben, präsentierte ein paar Weltneuheiten, die die ganze Automobilbranche beeinflußten. Der SLK macht da keine Ausnahme – bestes Beispiel ist sein neuartiges Variodach, das er auf Knopfdruck komplett im Heck versenken kann – so bekommt man zum Roadster ein vollwertiges Sportcoupé gratis dazu.
Vom Coupé zum Cabrio auf Knopfdruck. Innerhalb von 30 Sekunden verschwindet das Variodach vollständig im Kofferraum. Umgekehrt läßt sich der Roadster genauso bequem wieder in ein Coupé mit Stahldach verwandeln.
Größer, als man denkt: der Kofferraum des SLK.
Ganz untypisch für einen Roadster dieser Größe ist der großzügige Kofferraum des SLK. Bei geschlossenem Dach bringt er es auf immerhin 348 l Ladevolumen. Bei geöffnetem und im Kofferraum versenktem Dach stehen Ihnen immer noch 145 l Volumen zur Verfügung. Ein Rollo im Kofferraum trennt dabei säuberlich Ihr Gepäck vom Dach.

seiner konsequenten Sportlichkeit steckt in ihm die gesamte
Angesichts der eleganten Karosserie mag man gar nicht an Knautschzonen denken. Trotzdem sind Heck, Front und Seiten des SLK perfekt auf einen Aufprall vorbereitet.
cherheit: Knautschzonen, Gurtstraffer, Airbags und auf
bags. Selbst wenn man mal kein Dach über dem Kopf
an sich gut behütet. Die Verankerungen der A-Säulen sind
S LP 7685
Novum i
matisch
verhinde
wird, we
Studio m

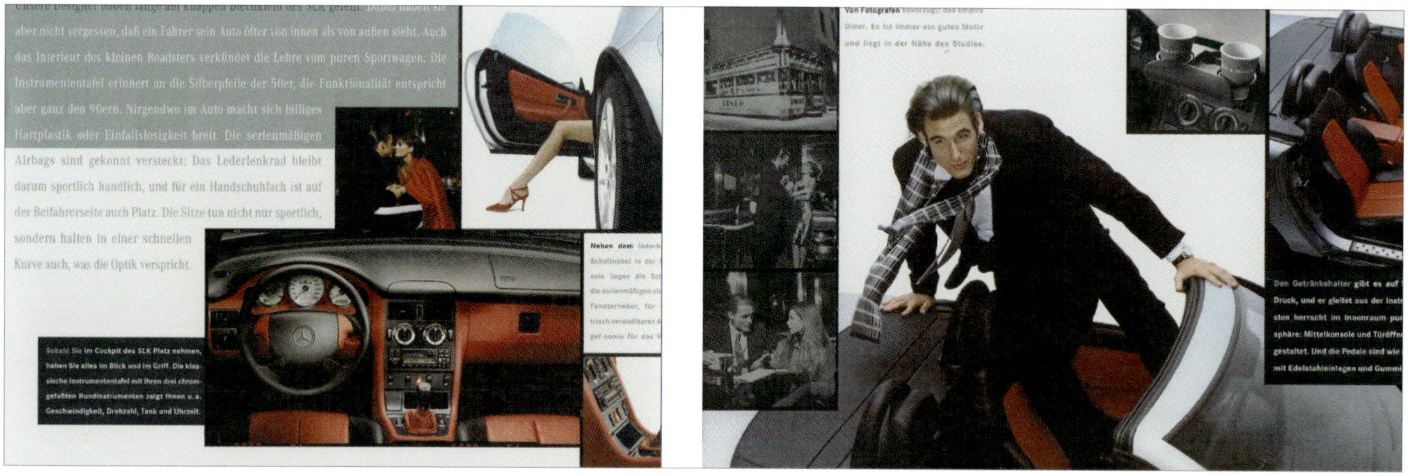
[illegible] aber nicht vergessen, daß ein Fahrer sein Auto öfter von innen als von außen sieht. Auch das Interieur des kleinen Roadsters verkündet die Lehre vom puren Sportwagen. Die Instrumententafel erinnert an die Silberpfeile der 50er, die Funktionalität entspricht aber ganz den 90ern. Nirgendwo im Auto macht sich billiges Hartplastik oder Einfallslosigkeit breit. Die serienmäßigen Airbags sind gekonnt versteckt: Das Lederlenkrad bleibt darum sportlich handlich, und für ein Handschuhfach ist auf der Beifahrerseite auch Platz. Die Sitze tun nicht nur sportlich, sondern halten in einer schnellen Kurve auch, was die Optik verspricht.
Sobald Sie im Cockpit des SLK Platz nehmen, haben Sie alles im Blick und im Griff. Die klassische Instrumententafel mit ihren drei chromgefaßten Rundinstrumenten zeigt Ihnen u. a. Geschwindigkeit, Drehzahl, Tank und Uhrzeit.

Die riesigen Scheinwerfer heizen
das Fotostudio zeitweise auf über
50 °C auf. Ungefähr bei der glei-
chen Temperatur wurde der SLK
schon vier Wochen lang durch
Death Valley gescheucht. Voll
ten und gut verhüllt vor
Härtetest überstehen. Ein
über sich ergehen lassen muß,

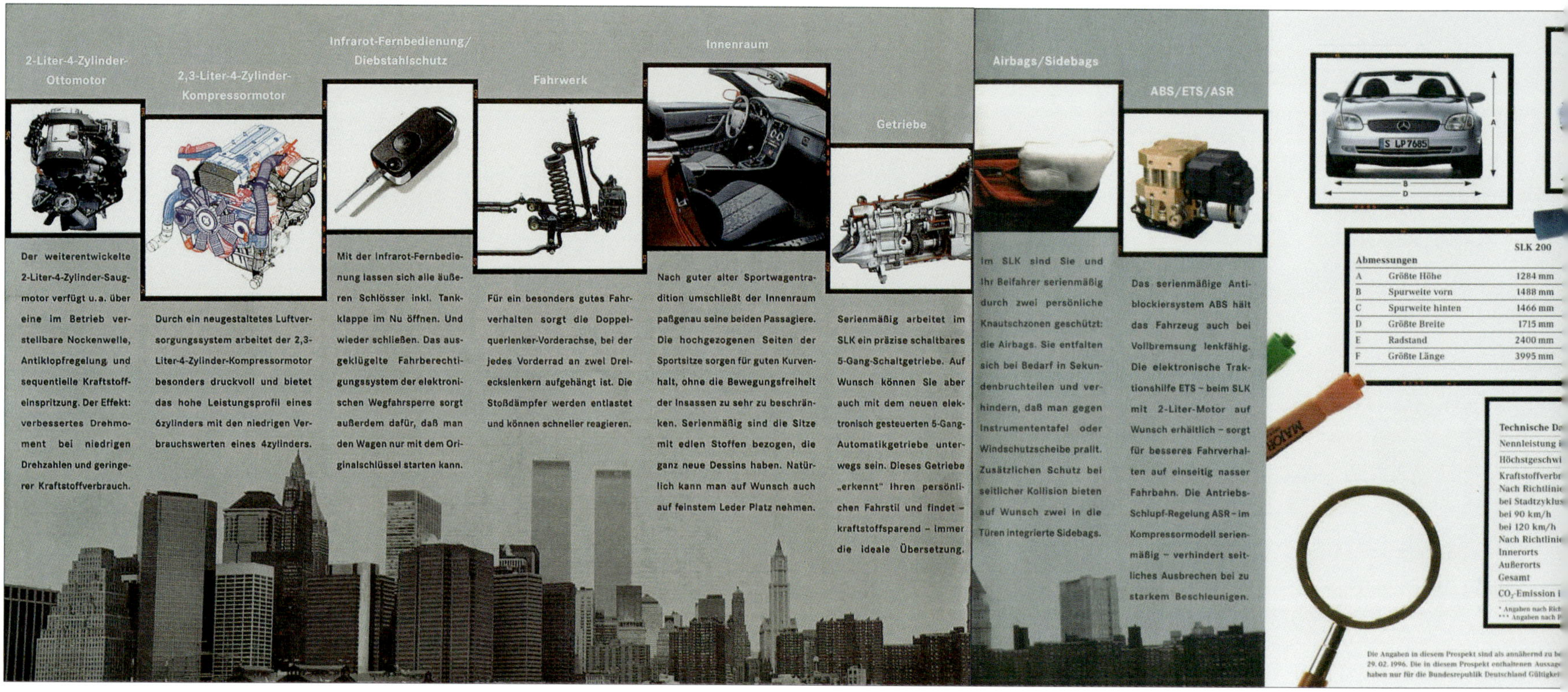
2-Liter-4-Zylinder-Ottomotor
Der weiterentwickelte 2-Liter-4-Zylinder-Saugmotor verfügt u. a. über eine im Betrieb verstellbare Nockenwelle, Antiklopfregelung und sequentielle Kraftstoffeinspritzung. Der Effekt: verbessertes Drehmoment bei niedrigen Drehzahlen und geringerer Kraftstoffverbrauch.
2,3-Liter-4-Zylinder-Kompressormotor
Durch ein neugestaltetes Luftversorgungssystem arbeitet der 2,3-Liter-4-Zylinder-Kompressormotor besonders druckvoll und bietet das hohe Leistungsprofil eines 6zylinders mit den niedrigen Verbrauchswerten eines 4zylinders.
Infrarot-Fernbedienung/Diebstahlschutz
Mit der Infrarot-Fernbedienung lassen sich alle äußeren Schlösser inkl. Tankklappe im Nu öffnen. Und wieder schließen. Das ausgeklügelte Fahrberechtigungssystem der elektronischen Wegfahrsperre sorgt außerdem dafür, daß man den Wagen nur mit dem Originalschlüssel starten kann.
Fahrwerk
Für ein besonders gutes Fahrverhalten sorgt die Doppelquerlenker-Vorderachse, bei der jedes Vorderrad an zwei Dreiecksienkern aufgehängt ist. Die Stoßdämpfer werden entlastet und können schneller reagieren.
Innenraum
Nach guter alter Sportwagentradition umschließt der Innenraum paßgenau seine beiden Passagiere. Die hochgezogenen Seiten der Sportsitze sorgen für guten Kurvenhalt, ohne die Bewegungsfreiheit der Insassen zu sehr zu beschränken. Serienmäßig sind die Sitze mit edlen Stoffen bezogen, die ganz neue Dessins haben. Natürlich kann man auf Wunsch auch auf feinstem Leder Platz nehmen.
Getriebe
Serienmäßig arbeitet im SLK ein präzise schaltbares 5-Gang-Schaltgetriebe. Auf Wunsch können Sie aber auch mit dem neuen elektronisch gesteuerten 5-Gang-Automatikgetriebe unterwegs sein. Dieses Getriebe „erkennt" Ihren persönlichen Fahrstil und findet – kraftstoffsparend – immer die ideale Übersetzung.
Airbags/Sidebags
Im SLK sind Sie und Ihr Beifahrer serienmäßig durch zwei persönliche Knautschzonen geschützt: die Airbags. Sie entfalten sich bei Bedarf in Sekundenbruchteilen und verhindern, daß man gegen Instrumententafel oder Windschutzscheibe prallt. Zusätzlichen Schutz bei seitlicher Kollision bieten auf Wunsch zwei in die Türen integrierte Sidebags.
ABS/ETS/ASR
Das serienmäßige Antiblockiersystem ABS hält das Fahrzeug auch bei Vollbremsung lenkfähig. Die elektronische Traktionshilfe ETS – beim SLK mit 2-Liter-Motor auf Wunsch erhältlich – sorgt für besseres Fahrverhalten auf einseitig nasser Fahrbahn. Die Antriebs-Schlupf-Regelung ASR – im Kompressormodell serienmäßig – verhindert seitliches Ausbrechen bei zu starkem Beschleunigen.
S LP 7685
SLK 200
Abmessungen
A Größte Höhe 1284 mm
B Spurweite vorn 1488 mm
C Spurweite hinten 1466 mm
D Größte Breite 1715 mm
E Radstand 2400 mm
F Größte Länge 3995 mm

Auf Wunsch erhalten Sie eine Klimaanlage (Tempmatik), die bei geschlossenem Dach für ein angenehmes Klima sorgt.
KOMPRESSOR
Es gibt verschiedene Formen von Hitze. Das Death Valley kennt sie alle: tropische Feuchtigkeit, beißende Sommersonne, dörre Wüstenhitze. Durch diese gigantische „Bratpfanne" mit ihren dampfenden Berggipfeln, den weitflächigen Gebirgsausläufern und den sengend heißen Ebenen führt die dreistündige Jungfernfahrt des SLK. Schon beim Start um 11.30 Uhr zeigt die Fahrmaschine, wie sie zu dieser Herausforderung steht: Kaum gezündet, läßt der Kompressor-aufgeladene Reihenvierzylinder einen bulligen Sound erklingen. Jetzt geht es erst einmal stur geradeaus bei gleichbleibendem Tempo von 55 mph. Schon bei diesem leichten Vorspiel bekommt man die direkte Lenkung und die magnetische Bodenhaftung angenehm zu spüren. Der SLK und sein Fahrer sind eins. Nach dem anschließenden Leerlauftest folgt das Jüngste Gericht: in schnellem Tempo bergauf, dann wieder kriechend bergab, schließlich monotones Stop and go. Hier zeigen Kupplung und Getriebe, was sie können: Kurze Pedalwege, schnelle und präzise Gangwechsel machen diese Höllentour mit dem SLK rundum zu einem sportlichen Vergnügen.
SLK 230
S LP 7685

S LP 7685
C
SLK 230 Kompressor
142/5300
231
10,8
5,9
7,6
12,5
6,6
8,8
208
Vorläufige, errechnete Werte.
und Lieferumfang bleiben vorbehalten. Stand per Redaktionsschluß am
gesetzliche, rechtliche und steuerliche Vorschriften und Auswirkungen
derausstattungen, die nicht zum serienmäßigen Lieferumfang gehören.

Fotograf Michel Comte
Model
Model
S LP 7685
S LP 7390

The following three pages show a series of ten alternative catalogue shots taken in America, with most of the static images taken in New York. The car is a normally-aspirated SLK200 model with European lighting and the standard wheels for that vehicle grade.

SLK 200
New Jersey
45 DTM
VEHICLE MFR

Canon
SAMSUNG
SUNTORY
WHISKY
W 46 ST
ONE WAY
QUALITY
AND
BEST MUSICAL REVIVAL
MARTINIQUE
JEWELERS
FRASIER

A pre-production SLK pictured with the 190SL.

Some of the first press pictures released of the new car, with S-LK 9608 serving as an SLK200 with optional alloys …

sales of 30,000 units worldwide (possibly 35,000 – the maximum that production facilities would allow), with conquest sales expected to make up a fair proportion of turnover. In other words, the marketing people were expecting to welcome a lot of customers that were new to the Mercedes-Benz brand rather than those already loyal to it, so the Porsche and BMW rivals from Germany, as well as those fielded by Italian makers, posed a far greater threat to the SLK's success than the Stuttgart firm had become accustomed to – the outcome of repeat business in established model lines is a great deal easier to predict than tackling a fresh market sector, and BMW had already snapped up 15,000 open car customers with the Z3 (pre-launched in late 1995 via the Nieman Marcus Christmas catalogue, tied-in with the *Goldeneye* Bond film), while Porsche was also keeping the Boxster name alive in adverts and advance press pictures – images were leaked in March 1996, well ahead of the 1996 Paris Salon launch, resulting in another 10,000 firm orders in place before deliveries of the new Porsche began in the early part of 1997.

Continued on page 98

... and also as an SLK230 Kompressor, depending on the angle ...

S LK 9608

Opposite page, above, and overleaf: The badging that gave the game away on the front wing was applied to the driver's side only, while rear-end shots were avoided taken at a distance on images purporting to be of the 2-litre car.

S LK 9608

Just to add to the confusion, another supercharged car wore the same number plates for some early PR shots.

SLK PRODUCTION

Beginning officially in July 1996 (a month later than originally forecast), production of the SLK took place in the Bremen plant, a factory originally established by the Borgward concern in 1938, but taken over by Daimler-Benz in 1971. Although the site was initially used by Mercedes for light commercial vehicles as well as estate versions of the W123, the 190 had been made there, and production of the SL moved there, too, as soon as the R107 series run came to an end, giving way to the R129 model. With the runaway success of the SLK at the time of its launch, an unprecedented third shift was put on duty, allowing for an absolute maximum of up to 50,000 cars a year to be made. Incidentally, it was Manfred Remmel who oversaw the production and material supplies side of things at this time. He was later appointed President of the Magna Steyr concern.

The Bremen plant, pictured here in 1998. Thanks to the success of the SLK, 600 new jobs were created there.

The pie was certainly there, but it was getting shared amongst a lot of hungry folks.

Of course, history tells us that the Mercedes hierarchy had no real cause for concern – the level of advance orders probably took even the most optimistic of officials by surprise, but there was no harm in playing the same game as the rivals, especially with so much at stake. Let's face it, the upfront investment required to build a modern automobile is quite staggering, and it's necesssary to be sure this will be recouped.

Photographs are one thing, but seeing a car in the flesh is something quite different, especially under harsh lighting. The advance orders had been placed by brand fanatics, and those who wanted to be seen with the latest fashion accessory. There was also an element of skullduggery in some sales, with people hoping to cash-in because where demand far outstripped supply. Those who viewed the car at Turin and other shows that followed over the ensuing months were either waiting to compare all the main rivals before making a purchase, or waiting to be captivated by the car's charm. Either way, these more levelheaded types were who needed convincing, and the ones who would make up the vast majority of customers in the future …

Initial press reaction

When it comes to capturing the mood of the moment, Rik Paul summed up the situation nicely with his report in the August

Above: A prototype manufacturing jig being reviewed. As well as ensuring pre-planned production sequences were feasible, this kind of upfront work also helped reduce costs and improve quality by making life on the production line easier. The jig is shown in operation, left.

The body starting to take shape, with high-precision locating pieces all the way along the production process to ensure accurate tolerances. Many of the panels were pressed at the famous Karmann works in Osnabrück, to the west of Hanover, with assembly taking place at the Bremen factory.

Despite the highly-automated nature of modern car building, there were still many areas in which hand welding and hand finishing were required. From here on, the roof assembly (supplied by CTS) would be added, and the paintwork done before chassis component modules were attached. Trimming then completed the production cycle, which typically took about 52 hours per car.

One of the SLK200 press cars that was made available for testing at the time of the Turin Show. This car tipped the scales at 1270kg (2794lb), which was some 55kg (121lb) lighter than the supercharged models.

1996 issue of *Motor Trend*: "Eye-popping yellow, brilliant blue, hot red: What's Mercedes-Benz coming to? It can be summed up in three letters: SLK. That's Mercedes' entry in the new wave of German roadsters, arriving fast on the heels of the BMW Z3 and in pace with the Porsche Boxster. Beyond the actual car, though, the SLK reflects the new, fresher-thinking, more daring attitude that's beginning to rise to the surface of the traditionally conservative automaker. And in the case of the SLK, that thinking goes much deeper than just the colourful paint … Our recent brief exposure to the car in Turin heightened our feelings that the SLK will be a mouth-watering addition to the Euro-roadster club."

Three months later, C Van Tune wrote in the same journal: "The wedge profile combines with the car's extremely short overhangs, husky 16-inch wheel and tyre package, and lack of ornamental gewgaws to produce a look that's at once upscale, sporty, youthful, and classic.

An SLK230 Kompressor that was featured in a *Motor Trend* article.

Above and opposite: A couple of views of an SLK200 with its top up and down – another vehicle from the press fleet. Note the 'SLK200' badge on the tail.

"Romp on the gas from a stop, and the SLK moves out smartly. You'll hear a slight howl from the supercharger during aggressive driving, though the exhaust is a bit too muted for our sporting tastes. The flat torque curve makes nipping and tucking through urban traffic a delight, as the engine doesn't have to scream at red-line to usher a hearty push in the back.

"On the ultra-twisty two-lanes that weave trough Tuscany, the car rewarded with a light, supple driving style and virtually neutral handling. The car's manners are unfetteringly competent, undeniably secure, unequivocally spirited. Dive into a turn and you'll discover brilliant steering response, outstanding balance, and virtually fade-free brakes. You'll need to switch off the

S LK 520

traction control to feel like Fangio in the Mille Miglia, but even the master would have trouble getting this car out of shape on a dare. The level of confidence it instills in mere mortals is godlike."

Voting the SLK to its 'Ten Best' list even before sales started, *Car & Driver* noted: "We've seen supercharged engines before. We've seen carbonfibre interior panels. We've even seen folding steel convertible tops before. But we've never seen these features, and more, wrapped in a lovely, agile package adorned with the three-pointed star on its hood.

"The SLK has the responsive performance and sharp handling we would expect from a tiny two-seater. It has the cozy interior implied by its small size combined with the classy execution expected from a Mercedes. Best of all, it has that wonderful top that transforms the car from a slick convertible – which, by the way, shakes and rattles less than any other flip-top in the world – to a no-compromises closed coupé. Despite the wondrous folding roof and its attendant mechanism, there's even a decent trunk.

"We are deeply disappointed that Mercedes has chosen not to offer the SLK with a manual gearbox. But even so, the SLK defines a new paradigm for sports cars – one that rivals will be chasing in the forthcoming years."

Other reports from Europe, Australasia and the Far East echoed the enthusiasm, with the car's playful looks, safe handling and practical packaging scoring high with the group of experienced journalists allowed to test the SLK long before it went on sale. The folks in Stuttgart must have had confidence in their new baby of course, otherwise this additional PR stunt could have backfired horribly. As it was, with the pages and pages of good press generated worldwide, the waiting lists simply grew still longer …

The home market

With the SLK making its proper debut in Italy, a price list was put together at the same time for the dealers in Germany. This first official price list, dated 23 April 1996, gives us an ideal overview of the standard specifications for the home market cars. The basic SLK200 was priced at DM 46,000 at this time, while the supercharged 2.3-litre model commanded DM 53,000. As with the options that follow, 15 per cent VAT had to be added to these

German advertising from 1996.

An early home market SLK in perfect open car country.

Domestic cars came as standard with the 'Tirefit' system, meaning a can of sealant and an electric pump that plugged into the cigarette lighter were supplied rather than a regular spare wheel. This saved almost 20kg (44lb), and freed up valuable luggage space as well. With punctures being quite rare in reality, this was probably an ideal option.

figures, but it was usual for base prices to be quoted minus any taxes, as the rate can change at any time, and is out of the control of the works.

Standard features on domestic models included alloy wheels; anti-lock brakes (ABS); power-assisted steering (PAS); the 'Tirefit' system (with an electric compressor and a can of sealant rather than a spare wheel); power-adjusted and heated door mirrors; repeater indicators; a third brakelight; front and rear foglights; parking lights; laminated windscreen; power windows with green-tinted glass all-round; a heated rear screen with timer; remote central locking with immobilizer and panic switch; cloth trim; seat occupancy recognition; sports seats with height adjustment on both sides; dual airbags; individual heater controls; an outside temperature gauge; digital clock; soft storage pockets in the doors and on the rear bulkhead; audio preparation (including an aerial under the bumper); a hazard

The optional cassette holder (SA code 331). This angle also gives a useful view of the seat adjustment knob on the backrest. Inset: The map pockets on the rear bulkhead.

warning triangle; a lights-on buzzer; first aid kit; a windblocker, and a locking luggage box in the boot. The supercharged car also had the ASR traction control system as standard, as well as a larger alloy wheel and tyre combination, and a rubber dressing piece on the rear wheelarch.

Regular options included an automatic transmission with cruise control (SA code 423, priced at DM 2990); metallic paint at DM 950; side airbags (292) at DM 650; a heated windscreen washer system (875) at DM 295; headlight washers (600) at DM 400; steering column adjustment (441) at DM 250; air-conditioning (580) at DM 2300; an alarm system (551) – which was DM 500, or DM 655 if upgraded with a towing protection facility (882); a cassette holder (331) at DM 80; a fire extinguisher (682) at DM 190; seat heaters (873) at DM 560; leather trim, priced at DM 1700, and a luggage rack (726) at DM 100. With a fully-loaded car – especially one with things like seat heating –

The roof rack (SA code 726), suitable for skis, surfboards, bicycles and the like, sat on the A-post and rear wings, just below the C-pillar, thus avoiding the roof.

A cupholder and coin box insert was a no-cost option (code 309), taking the place of the regular box provided for sunglasses and the like. Cupholders are a must for the US market, but not as popular in European cars, especially those of a sporting ilk.

Telephones were still an expensive option at this time. Note also the 'Exquisit' stereo unit, and the switch for the seat heaters in the background.

an uprated battery (SA code 673), rated at 74Ah rather than the standard 62Ah, needed to be specified, adding DM 105 to the invoice.

No-cost options (NCO) included a spacesaver spare (SA code 669, replacing the 'Tirefit' system and luggage box), and a cupholder insert (309). Options that were unique to each model included the 16-inch alloys fitted to the Kompressor model for the normally-aspirated machine (SA code 642, priced at DM 800 plus tax, and coming complete with a rubber lip on the rear arches), the ETS traction control system for the SLK200 (code 212, also listed at DM 800), and all-weather tyres (code 645), priced at DM 205 on the 2-litre car, or as an NCO on the SLK230 Kompressor. There were also the AMG options, with the 772 bodykit priced at DM 6900 for both cars, although the 17-inch wheel and tyre set (794) was priced at DM 3300 on the SLK200, which was DM 800 more than if the same alloys were specified on the larger-engined machine.

On the audio and communication front, there was the MB Classic RDS radio/cassette unit (515) at DM 780, the MB Spezial RDS radio/cassette (512) at DM 1130, the MB Exquisit RDS

Another early German-registered SLK230 Kompressor, but this one featuring 'Merope' 16-inch alloys and full stainless treadplates, both of which could be bought from the dealer as accessories.

The attractive 'Erakis' 15-inch alloys, available from dealers rather than a factory-fitted option.

Seatcovers were listed as another accessory, but it's doubtful whether many sets were ever sold.

radio/cassette (510) at DM 1780, and the Spezial with a CD slot rather than a cassette player (755) at DM 1230. All these came with four speakers and an amplifier, although this setup could be bought as a separate option (SA code 533) for DM 330; one could also upgrade to a Bose sound system (810) for DM 950. As for telephones, there was a 'Handy' unit (313), or a 'Standard' phone (314), both of which were about DM 1850 once the wiring had been added in, while a tail-mounted antenna (270) added DM 250 to the invoice.

There was also an accessory catalogue issued for SLK users and fans, with all manner of goodies for the car and fashion items for ladies and gentlemen, including things like diecast models, sunglasses, T-shirts, tie-clips, watches, and bags.

Auto, Motor und Sport tested a manual SLK230 Kompressor model in September 1996 – one of the first proper road tests of the model, as sales had officially only just started on 14 September – and rated it very highly. In fact, maximum points were scored in five of the six categories, and the odd remaining one only just missed out on a top score. Although the kerb weight was a long way above the 1200kg (2640lb) target originally set in 1993, the 0-60 time of 7.2 seconds and top speed of 144mph (230kph) was impressive enough, but the 26.4mpg (Imperial) average fuel economy was simply stunning for a car in this class.

A domestic SLK230 Kompressor ...

By March 1997, the price of the basic SLK200 had increased to DM 47,400, with that of the SLK230 Kompressor rising to DM 54,400 at the same time. This represented a price hike of around three per cent, although virtually all of the option prices remained unchanged. Indeed, about the only significant changes were those applied to the audio choices, with the basic 'Classic' radio being deleted, a reduction in price on the two 'Spezial' models (pricing now started at DM 800 instead of DM 1130), and the addition of a CD holder for the centre cubby (SA code 330), listed at DM 80.

Changes to specification included side airbags as standard, the cost of the former option accounting for a fair bit of the price increase, and a warning chime for when the handbrake had been left on. The rubber lip on the wheelarch of cars fitted with 16-inch wheels was no longer listed as a feature, although a few cars continued to sport them.

The American market

The United States was always going to provide Mercedes-Benz with a huge market for the SLK, as had been the tradition with sporting models emanating from Europe since the end of the Second World War. Sales officially began in March 1997, with the SLK classed as an early 1998 MY machine. However, with Stateside sales restricted to around 6000 units for the first year, the waiting list quickly stretched to 12 months and beyond – demand far outstripping supplies in the early days, meaning the 1998 tag was probably quite an accurate description for most buyers.

Americans were initially restricted to the SLK230 Kompressor model with automatic transmission only. This wasn't a big surprise, given US emission control requirements, as ECT programmes can mask a lot of things that a manual car, with heavier on/off throttle inputs, can't do as easily. Some quarters expressed

... at speed!

disappointment that a manual wasn't available, especially as the car's looks got the enthusiast's pulse racing. But the SLK was a sporting car, not a pure sports car, and modern automatics are a far cry from the slushboxes of yore.

Priced at $39,700, this put the SLK in the Porsche Boxster arena, and around $10,000 up on the American-built BMW Z3. Saying that, the Benz was very well equipped, with even the most demanding of customers wanting for little. Standard equipment included variable-focus halogen headlights with washer system; front and rear foglights; heated power door mirrors; power windows with tinted glass all-round (including a heated glass rear window); a detachable draft deflector; 16-inch aluminium alloy wheels; ABS braking; traction control; PAS with a leather-trimmed steering wheel and telescopic adjustment; air-conditioning with separate left/right controls; cruise control; full analogue instrumentation combined with a digital clock; outside temperature gauge and oddometers; dual front and side airbags; a central armrest with storage facility to augment the oddments space provided in the centre console and door pockets; courtesy lighting; two-tone leather trim; velour carpeting and SLK floormats; infrared power central locking with an integrated alarm system; a universal garage door opener, and a 'Special' radio/cassette unit mated to the six-speaker Bose sound system. At this stage, the only options were metallic paint at $600, heated seats at $595, and a couple of packages combining a mobile phone and trunk-mounted CD-changer unit (the stereo pre-wired to accept the latter), the cheapest version being $1495.

Did the SLK live up to all the hype? After driving the first US-spec car to hit American shores, flown into the country specially with its 160mph speedometer and tiny marker lights on the front bumper (the latter a feature unique to the US market), Patrick Bedard concluded that the SLK was not really a sports car: "Sports cars this size are frisky critters, turning every drive into a cavort. The SLK, on the other hand, feels responsible, even circumspect, in normal driving. It delivers measured responses to your touch, more like a grown-up sedan … It's too refined to be crammed into the sports car definition. When the roof is up, this roadster is shake-free, draft-free, and roar-free in the manner of the best grand touring car, and GTs were always thought to be too well-mannerly to be genuine sports cars. Then, too, there is the transmission – an automatic five-speed is the only choice. Real sports cars, even in this Pentium age, still have gears changed by stubby levers."

You could be forgiven for thinking the *Car & Driver* man wasn't all that impressed, but he summed up the car as "a smile on wheels, guaranteed to send both friends and strangers into deep envy." The SLK may not have been a pure sports car in Bedard's eyes, but the "serious, expert, handling behaviour" was held up as being something special, even if the tyres tramlined. Above all, the car succeeded in completely fulfilling its design brief. Testers often forget to factor in the target audience, but Bedard zoomed right in on them. He even created a new sales sector name for the machine – while the SUV is a sport utility vehicle, he classed the SLK as a CUTE, standing for a 'clever utility two-seat express.' As a CUTE, the little Benz cornered the market.

Bedard's colleague, Barry Winfield, echoed this observation: "I expected the baby SL to be like Mazda's Miata and BMW's Z3 – compact, nippy, and fun-to-drive. What I didn't expect was for the SLK to be a faithful interpretation of the SL theme – to have the solidity, poise, and manner of the bigger, more expensive cars. But it does. The SLK has a much stiffer structure than any of the other small roadsters I've driven, and a ride that belies its short wheelbase. Yet it still steers with keen accuracy, and handles with a kind of controlled athleticism. I guess you do get what you pay for."

Of the other *Car & Driver* staffers, while Don Schroeder was waiting for the Boxster to arrive, Fred Gregory declared he wanted an SLK for himself: "What's not to like about this car? It looks terrific, drives great, and I could spend hours watching the top go up and down."

Tipping the scales at 1370kg (3014lb), with 53 per cent of the weight over the front wheels, the 191bhp/206lbft (SAE nett) SLK covered the 0-60 yardstick in 7.2 seconds, and went on to dismiss the quarter-mile mark 8.3 seconds later. The magazine recorded a top speed of 139mph (222kph) before the governor kicked in, and pulled 0.86g on the skidpan with moderate understeer from the Michelin rubber. Interestingly, later tests pegged the car as being much quicker, with one magazine achieving a 0-60 time of 6.6 seconds, although it should be noted that another independent test recorded 7.6. In view of that, perhaps 7.2 is about right.

As spring arrived, we started getting the articles everyone had been waiting for – the SLK in a pitched battle against the 201bhp (SAE) Porsche Boxster and 189bhp (SAE) BMW Z3, the latter now sporting a 2.8-litre six at the front-end. The first to put the three German newcomers together was *Road & Track* in its March 1997 issue.

After driving the three cars – all within a $38,325-$45,775 price range as tested – with the 1436kg (3160lb) Benz sitting in the middle, Douglas Knott wasn't so happy with the automatic gearbox, and added: "There are other things about the SLK that don't enthral me. The steering, though quick by Mercedes standards and possessing the sort of undemanding straight-line stability that makes cruising the Interstate a pleasure, is a bit stingy with information about the road-tyre interface. [And] its engine sounds coarse when heard back-to-back with the pleasing mechanical repartee of the Boxster and Z3 powerplants.

"So the SLK is not a sports car in the truest sense – yet I'm captivated by this car as a whole, smitten by its engineering, appreciative of its styling, and respectful of its performance. In this last area, this smallest Mercedes is, at most, a mere half-second in arrears of both the Boxster and Z3 in the critical 0-60mph and quarter-mile acceleration tests; in braking, the Merc bests the BMW from 80mph and 60mph, and more than holds its own against the Boxster. And what the SLK lacks in steering feedback, it makes up for in the ultra-stable, unflappable way it tracks through corners.

"The stiff structure no doubt contributes to the stable handling feel and the remarkably good ride, where there's a comforting sense that all inputs are being absorbed by the shocks, not the car's structure."

After two days of testing, the conclusion was: "For the purist, the pick would have to be the Boxster [the most expensive of the bunch]. For the traditionalist, perhaps only the Z3 would

The German tuning companies were quick to get in on the act, as these adverts from Lorinser and Brabus clearly show.

do. And for the enthusiast who places ingenuity and comfort slightly ahead of all-out sportiness, the SLK is an excellent choice. To overlook any of these enticing Germans would truly be a shame."

The *Car & Driver* test in the following month was a little less flattering. It was the most frugal of the three, the quietest of the three, the best in the braking, skidpan and emergency lane change tests, but ultimately scored a total of 91 points – one less than the BMW, and four less than the Porsche. The main gripe came with the lack of a manual gearbox and subdued chassis feedback, both of which are of paramount importance if one is judging a pure sports car, and that was how the SLK was viewed in this particular test. With a little more absolute control and involvement, the result would have been quite different, but the conclusion read: "What you get is the best of both the coupé and convertible worlds, and a painless transition between the two, a state of excellence no true sports car has yet to match. Whereas we're firm in our conviction that the SLK comes up short as a sports car, we're also aware that the majority of wanna-owns prefer it that way."

Later in the year, *Motor Trend* put an SLK back-to-back with a 1971 280SL, which gives a fascinating comparison, as the concept was much the same – a comfortable, more refined sporting machine rather than a pure sports car. Even with an SL in tow, the SLK was still attracting attention, that's for sure. As Rik Paul noted at the end of the article: "Drive one down the boulevard and the turning heads will have you wondering if there are any other sports cars on the street."

The right-hookers

The British market had always been loyal to the Mercedes-Benz brand for decades, so right-hand drive cars with the three-pointed star up the front were a common sight. Having the steering wheel and pedal set on the opposite side to the German cars (and the necessary reworking of odd components that came with the change), was about the only difference of note compared to the home market machines, as the centre console and handbrake position was carried over, as well as the same indicator wand. On saying that, the light switch found its way to the opposite side of the steering column, a 160mph speedo was used, like that seen on US cars, and the wipers parked on the opposite side of the windscreen in a thoughtful gesture to complete the package.

Articles released at the time of the 1996 Turin Show pointed towards a US-style vehicle for the UK – a 2.3-litre supercharged car with an automatic gearbox only, with a 2-litre NA machine perhaps following late in 1997. Delivery forecasts noted November 1996 for the first of the 1400 cars allocated to the British Isles to start drifting through, each expected to carry a sticker price of "under £30,000."

By the time the SLK made its UK public debut at the British International Motor Show on 18 October 1996 (the earlier dates were press and trade days), the waiting list had already extended to two years. Mercedes-Benz occupied stand number 222 at the NEC, with a yellow SLK230 Kompressor gracing the turntable. Priced at £29,500, the announcement that UK deliveries were to be delayed slightly did nothing to dampen the enthusiasm generated by the car. I can well remember my best friend seriously looking into the prospect of ownership, even making enquiries in Holland to jump the queue.

Not long after, *Autocar* arranged for a testmatch between an automatic SLK230 Kompressor and a manual Porsche Boxster. With the first of the UK cars expected about the same time as BMW Z3 and Porsche Boxster in January 1997, this was more of a preview than a full test, using German-registered vehicles. The conclusion was interesting, nonetheless: "The SLK is the sportiest and most able Mercedes since the 190 Cossie, but it is no match for the Porsche. Its makers never intended it to be so. That it undercuts and outperforms the SL280 by £25,000 makes it all the more desirable. The Mercedes SLK is a car that will give enormous pleasure 365 days of the year, whatever the climate."

By November, Mercedes-Benz UK had got its first press car on the road. *MotorSport*'s Andrew Frankel was trying to put his finger on why the SLK was such a runaway success when no-one had even driven the car, and specifications were hard-pushed to eclipse those of rivals. He concluded: "What has hooked the buying public, enough to lend credibility to stories of new right-hand drive cars changing hands at £45,000, is its styling. Not only will you find in its lines the definitive template for the 21st century roadster, its shape is also remarkably faithful to the abiding traditions of its marque. And be it by luck or design, the timing of the SLK's appearance could hardly have worked better.

Brilliant advertising announcing the arrival of the SLK in Britain.

At once it makes the MGF seem a little bland, the Z3 a touch contrived and the Porsche Boxster even a little ugly.

"The SLK's proportions work in any light, from any angle, on the page and in the flesh. The cabin is as stylish as its exterior, taking extant Mercedes cues with its switchgear, ergonomics and driving position, and then adding its own touches – chromed surrounds for the instruments, unique dials and even a handbrake."

All fired up, Frankel was a little disappointed with the driving experience, though, largely because of the lack of a manual gearbox. While countries like America and Japan are quite happy with automatic transmissions, European enthusiasts tend to like feeling more involved when it comes to sporting models. Notwithstanding, the large spread of torque made progress effortless, and that side of the car's nature was always going to appeal to the majority of drivers, as opposed to the diehard who likes keeping the motor turning close to the red-line at every opportunity. One should also bear in mind that the heydays of motoring had already passed – heavier traffic, lower speed limits everywhere, often enforced by a growing band of cameras, and the idea of carefree wind-in-the-hair driving on open roads without another soul in sight was closer to the world of advertising agencies than the real world. Yes, it's nice to enjoy a well set up pure sports car on a race track, with a multitude of visceral sensations, but from personal experience, these cars are rarely much fun in everyday use. If anything, they're usually

A selection of some of the first proper UK press pictures, as opposed to shots of home market cars with British number plates.

frustrating. In that respect, the Benz engineers had tried to strike a balance between something that was useful enough to commute with but interesting enough to enjoy, and the convertible element simply added another string to the bow without any hassle – no hardtop to store, and no fears of parking outside at night.

To categorize a vehicle on its appearance is the mistake many testers made at the time of the SLK's debut, a problem exacerbated by the fact that so many articles worldwide were written by the same people, with their own particular viewpoint and expectations. A Rolls-Royce Corniche has two doors and a drophead, but that doesn't mean it's trying to be a sports car, no more than the heavyweight SL was. There are vehicles that look like proper sports cars with less go than the author on a Monday morning, and handling that matches that of a shopping trolley. Likewise, a Ford Escort Mk III RS1600i doesn't look like a sports car, but it certainly goes like one. Horses for courses.

We have to know what the design team was striving for, judge if they succeeded or not, and then add in a value-for-money element based on what else is available within the targeted market sector.

Frankel hit the nail on the head by stating: "The SLK's dreams are of the open road, tackled at speed but with maximum relaxation and economy of effort. Drive like this and it is truly captivating. Ride quality is unreasonably good ... Wind management, for those under six foot, is impressive, too. You hear a surprising amount of wind disturbance but feel practically none with the roof down."

Autocar tested the same vehicle, liking the "no-compromise folding steel roof, sleek styling, classy interior, storming performance, and superb build quality," but was less enamoured with the "poor fuel consumption, uncommunicative steering, and firm low-speed ride." There was no question regarding the performance, as the car showed itself capable of covering the 0-60 dash in 7.4 seconds and having a top speed of 140mph (224kph), and personally, in view of this, an average of 25.2mpg doesn't seem unreasonable, especially when one considers how hard test cars are pushed. However, combining this average with the small fuel tank, the testers felt compelled to point out the poor touring range, and that's fair enough, especially as the 40.4mpg cruising figure in the official paperwork was a good 30 per cent better than the best the *Autocar* guys could muster after going through seven tanks of petrol.

An interesting observation was made in the performance category: "Our only regret is that the SLK doesn't always feel as fast as the figures prove it to be. Blame this on the standard automatic five-speed gearbox, which changes ratios so quickly and smoothly under full throttle that the sensation of speed becomes muted. It's not quite so slick on kickdown, and the staggered gate design discourages you from resorting to manual override. Overall, though, it's a fine combination, and we can't see anyone being upset that a manual gearbox isn't offered in the UK." It was also noted that the "SLK chassis is short on low-speed thrills, but high on grip, stability and safety. Not even a heavy right foot can shake the SLK's tail."

Summing up, the magazine stated: "It looks and feels like a million dollars, yet it costs no more than a well-equipped Ford Scorpio. The second big selling point is the ease with which it fits into people's lives. Other than the obvious limiting factor of only having two seats, there really is no compromise. That is why people who would never previously have considered buying a two-seat soft top have no qualms about driving an SLK." After noting that the engine was not particularly exciting and the chassis was less talented than that of a Porsche Boxster: "if you can live with this, then the SLK will never disappoint."

UK sales started officially in January 1997, with the SLK230 Kompressor commanding £30,090. Most things were standard, including the 5AT, traction control, an alarm/immobilizer, and side airbags. Of the major options, metallic paint cost an extra £650, leather trim £1000, air-conditioning £1400, telescopic steering adjustment £130, and a radio/cassette unit £670.

The SLK fell into insurance group 17, which seemed rather steep, but the steel top must have helped keep it's ranking down a touch. It was still the same price at the end of the year, starring in a Mercedes-Benz range that started at £17,000 for the A-Class and went all the way up to £107,840 for the CL600 – the CL-Class having come about after the S-Class coupés were face-lifted in the summer of 1996. As for competitors, the contemporary Porsche Boxster 2.5 was listed at £33,950, while the Mazda MX-5 1.8 commanded £15,410, the BMW Z3 2.8 £28,120, and the Alfa Spider 2.0 £23,059.

In Japan, SLK sales began in early February, but an 18-month waiting list quickly built up. As with the US and UK markets, only an automatic version of the SLK230 Kompressor was available, although one could choose between lhd or rhd. It may seem odd, but while right-hand drive is the norm in Japan, left-hookers hold a special kudos, as it's obvious that the car has been imported. Anyway, other than the steering, about the only other options were the trim material and coachwork colour, for ¥4,900,000 bought a fully-loaded car, with side airbags, seat heaters and the Bose stereo coming as part of the package. Mercedes prices ranged from ¥3,900,000 for the C200 saloon to ¥17,200,000 for the CL600 coupé at this time, incidentally, with the SLK costing about the same as a C230 saloon.

Car Graphic compared an SLK with an automatic Porsche Boxster S in the spring. If the specs were brought closer together, there was a big difference in the cost of the two rivals in Japan, with the Zuffenhausen car costing ¥7,150,000 as tested. It was noted that the SLK felt quick and heavy at the same time (the magazine recorded a 0-60 time of 7.3 seconds, and a 15.1

Advertising from the time of the SLK's launch in Japan.

An SLK featured on the cover of the April 1997 edition of *Car Graphic* magazine. Note the lighting arrangements, which were much the same as on UK cars.

standing-quarter). The supercharger was appreciated in everyday use but, unlike the Boxster, the engine lacked the drama expected from a sports car. The SLK displayed exceptional stability for a car with such a short wheelbase, though. With the traction control switched off, the tester was able to explore the limits to a greater extent, but the Benz was still endowed with very safe handling – one needed to deliberately provoke the car into oversteer situations. The functional interior was praised, and the draft stopper worked well. In this particular match, the Benz won on the grounds of it being a reasonably-priced convertible and coupé wrapped into one.

Australia's *Wheels* magazine carried out the same test in its January 1997 issue. It was noted that the wide spread of torque and automatic gearbox on the SLK would hold strong appeal for "drivers who want to cruise in effortless, roofless serenity," while the Boxster needed constant attention to keep it on the boil – rewarding for motoring fans of a sporting bent, but tiresome for those with less enthusiasm for pushing a car hard just for the fun of it.

The handling setup was quite different, too, with the Benz feeling "rock solid, its controls heavier, more deliberate than the Porsche. You know the SLK will never deviate from its chosen line. Push it hard and gradually it begins to understeer, just enough to let you know that the Merc engineers didn't aspire to the same dynamic heights as those from Weissach. You naturally drive the Boxster harder and faster than the SLK."

The four-seater C208 CLK coupé made an excellent stablemate for the SLK, although a convertible version was sold from the spring of 1998, allowing those with families to enjoy open car motoring in style.

The article continued: "The interior is pure Mercedes-Benz; clever and practical with too many pouches and bins to mention here. It's a lovely place. In contrast, the Porsche – instruments apart – is disappointingly bland. No doubt the SLK is going to be the easiest sports car in the world to own. It's perfectly suited to the demands of its clients."

As for the conclusion: "Travelling in convoy, swapping from car to car, is the best possible way to discover relative merits and character. It's no cop-out to say both are brilliant. It's a choice between motoring priorities, not a question of superiority ... Different cars for different customers."

Available in right-hand drive guise with automatic transmission only, the SLK230 Kompressor went on sale as the next issue of *Wheels* hit the newsstands. Listed at $98,500 with air-conditioning as standard, it dropped in the middle of the C-Class price range, and at the entry-level in the E-Class series (the latter models starting at $90,900). It was half the cost of an SL280, but twice that of a Mazda MX-5, and just a fraction cheaper than the $109,995 being asked for a basic Porsche Boxster.

Meanwhile

With all the hype surrounding the SLK, including a fair few awards, it was easy to forget that major Mercedes-related events were happening in the background. The Brake Assist (BAS) safety system had been announced in November 1996, made standard on the S-Class and SL initially, but it was soon adopted on other vehicle lines. Developed by Daimler-Benz and Lucas Industries, this system measured the speed and force with which the brake pedal was applied, and if an emergency stop was detected, increased braking force up to the maximum the ABS system would allow.

The sporty two-door CLK coupé (C208) was announced at the 1997 Detroit Show. Based on the C-Class, it resembled the concept car displayed at the Geneva Show way back in 1993, and would go on to be immensely popular, helping to push annual passenger car production up to 726,686 units. The tin-top version was joined by a convertible model in March 1998.

Klaus-Dieter Vöhringer took the place of Hartmut Weule as the head of the R&D section at about the same time as the CLK was unveiled, while the E280 and E320 models that made their debut in Amsterdam in February were the first vehicles to make use of the all-new M112 V6 engines, featuring three valves per cylinder and twin ignition. A new generation of 4MATIC was also announced, with permanent four-wheel drive. In the following month, it was the turn of the new A-Class to take a bow in Geneva, where the SLK picked up the 'Cabrio Of The Year' award, selected by an international jury.

The business was restructured again in April 1997, when Mercedes-Benz AG merged into Daimler-Benz AG. More importantly, the new vee-engine plant in Bad Cannstatt (touted as the "factory of the future") was officially opened at the same time, allowing the production of M112 and M113 units in an efficient and eco-friendly manner. The one-millionth engine was built there just three years later.

The CLK-GTR homologation special was also presented in April, featuring a V12 engine and a lightweight carbonfibre body. Only 25 were built, but it was enough to qualify the car for the FIA GT Championships – a series that the model would quickly go on to dominate.

May 1997, and another new vehicle range was launched in the shape of the M-Class SUV, which was initially built in America. The C-Class cars were given a mild face-lift the following month, and more models were added to the line at the Frankfurt Show in September, alongside a selection of fresh E-Class variants.

Finally, the 1997 Tokyo Show was selected as the venue to present the Maybach luxury saloon concept vehicle. It would eventually go into production, thus reviving a treasured name from the past in mid-2002.

The 1998 season proper

By the time the 1998 MY rolled around, a few production changes had already been made to the SLK. Almost before the first batch of cars had started arriving at dealerships, the alternator on the SLK 200 was changed from a Bosch unit to a Valeo one, and the flywheel, ignition coils and HFM control module were modified soon after. The automatic transmission control module was revised on the SLK230 Kompressor model in the summer of 1996, with the engine control module changed about nine months later.

During the latter part of spring 1997, all SLKs benefited from new rear brake calipers, fresh sparkplugs, a new oil pump, and fanbelt tensioner. A new header rail was also adopted, where the roof panel met the windscreen. With progress waiting for no man, Brake Assist brought about the need for a new brake servo and master cylinder. In addition, the supercharged car gained a new exhaust manifold, although the 2-litre NA machine inherited one a few months later, along with a modified oxygen sensor unit and crank position sensor.

In Germany, the price list issued in September 1997 held few surprises, with the basic car prices carried over from March.

COLOUR & TRIM GUIDE

There were very few changes on the paint and trim side of things until February 2000, when the face-lifted car arrived, so it's easier to chart them in one block. Please remember that the more exciting interior options are usually distinctive two-tone colour schemes.

Standard paintwork options

Black (040), Polar White, also known as Arctic White (149), Imperial Red (582), and Yellowstone, aka Sunburst Yellow (685). Polar White was replaced by Firn White, aka Glacier White (143) in May 1997, and Imperial Red was superseded by Magma Red (586) in August 1998.

Metallic paintwork options

Green-Black, aka Emerald Black or Black Opal (189), Vivianite Green, aka Calypso Green (279), Linarite Blue, aka Bahama Blue (352), and Brilliant Silver (744). Green-Black was replaced by Obsidian Black (197) in August 1998, and Bernstein Red (aka Amber Red or Firemist Red, code 548) was added as an additional colour at the same time.

Interior trim options

Anthracite (aka Charcoal) cloth (021) or leather (221), Mondrian Blue (aka Navy) cloth (022) or leather (222), Mint Green cloth (026), Quartz (aka Oyster) leather (225), and Scarlet Red (aka Salsa) cloth (027) or leather (227).

The full colour palette for the first SLKs.

Brake Assist (BAS) had been added to the SLK's spec sheet in the summer of 1997, and Assyst was another new feature, the onboard computer working out more flexible and sensible servicing schedules based on an owner's driving style and mileage. A small spanner symbol and the required servicing information would pop up occasionally in the odometer section of the LCD displays, reminding the driver that maintenance was due or recommended. ASR became an option on the SLK200 (SA code 471, priced at DM 1200), taking the place of the old ETS option, but continuing as standard on the supercharged car. On the paintwork side, metallic paint continued as a DM 950 option, with Designo paint (standard metallic, Varicolour or LCP types) varying from between DM 2600 and DM 9200. Equally, standard leather trim continued at DM 1700, while Designo leather (monotone or two-tone) commanded DM 3700. It was also possible to specify Designo leather trim for the roll-over bars (DM 1050), the centre console (DM 1150), and the special Designo sports seats (DM 5300).

The SLK's five-speed automatic gearbox was revised at the end of 1997, and the timing chain tensioning mechanism was overhauled on the M111 engine at the beginning of 1998. As spring rolled around, the windscreen washer pump and reservoir were changed, followed by the door shells, boot lid panel and seatbelts.

Base car prices increased by DM 1100 on the SLK200, and DM 800 on

A 1998 MY German market SLK with the AMG appendages and wheels.

The domestic SLK200 for the 1998 season.

An early 1998 SLK that has been given the Designo treatment, with special leather on the seats, door trim, roll-over hoops, steering wheel and centre console. Note also the contrasting stitching on the gearlever and the AMG monoblock wheels fitted to this car.

This is how the US-spec SLK230 Kompressor model looked from 1998 onwards, with a radio mast on the rear wing. The unique lighting for the American market, with markers on the trailing edge of the front bumper inserts, can also be seen in this picture. (Courtesy Wikimedia Commons)

the SLK230 Kompressor in April 1998. At the same time, German VAT went from 15 per cent to 16 per cent (the rate in force until January 2007, as it happens), so there was a double whammy on the bottom line of the invoice. As compensation, the ASR system was made standard on both SLK grades. In addition, the old 882 towing protection option was integrated into the alarm, which continued as a DM 500 extra as before, thus saving DM 155 for the security conscious. A garage door opener (SA code 231, priced at DM 350) was new for Germany, as was a DM 450 automatic anti-dazzle mirror option (code 249, applying to both inner and outer mirrors). The radios and telephones were changed at this time, with new fibre optic connections the main difference. The 'Spezial' became the MB Audio 10 (code 756 with a CD player or 753 without one), and the 'Exquisit' became the MB Audio 30 (code 750); prices were carried over on each equivalent. As for the phones, the 314 option was replaced by a 316 version, and the 313 became either a 312 or 317. All other options remained unchanged.

In America, too, everything was carried over from the first price list for the 1998 season. About the only change of note was a new radio aerial for US cars, with the original (hidden in the bumper) replaced by a mast fitted on the driver's-side rear wing. This may have deviated from the car's looks a little, but at least the complaints regarding poor radio reception in the States stopped overnight.

Motor Trend noted: "The SLK230 probably does the best job in the [Mercedes] line of bridging the gap between daily commuting and twisty backroad excitement. Its handling is beyond reproach …" Indeed, the famous magazine found that the little Benz could cut through its slalom test quicker than the new Corvette.

As for the major right-hand drive markets, there were no changes in Britain or Japan, although Australia gained the 2-litre normally-aspirated model in December 1997. A late decision had been made on this, but Australian buyers suddenly found themselves in the unusual position of having two SLKs in the line-up, albeit both with automatic transmission.

An American advert from the summer of 1998 featuring a Lorinser SLK with 18-inch wheels, and a bodykit that reminds the author of the original Turin Show concept car.

On the corporate front, the company opened its third Advanced Design Studio outside Germany in February 1998, this time in Como, Italy. The others had been established in Irvine (CA) in the States in 1991, and in Yokohama, Japan, during the following year.

The first of the 'Smart' microcars were presented shortly after in the spring of 1998, although sports car fans were far more interested in the face-lifted SL range, announced at the Turin Show that April. As it happens, the cost of SLK motoring went up in Germany that month, with the SLK200 going up from DM 56,260 including taxes to DM 56,956, while the supercharged model went from DM 64,032 to DM 64,728.

In the first week of May 1998, news broke of one of the biggest merger deals in the history of the motor industry, as America's Chrysler Corporation joined forces with Daimler-Benz AG to form a new company called DaimlerChrysler AG. The merger was approved at an EGM for shareholders in September, and completed in November. Jürgen Schrempp now shared the Chairman's post with Robert Eaton.

The W220 S-Class was launched at the 1998 Paris Salon, with the company's huge new proving grounds at Papenburg opening for business at around the same time. With the workforce now standing at over 440,000 people, passenger car production had hit a staggering 947,517 units in 1998.

Swansong

Following the April 1998 price increases in Germany, other than the addition of a small net in the passenger-side footwell and a 'Speedtronic' limiter feature being added to the 'Tempomat' cruise control system in mid-1998, nothing else of note happened with regard to the SLK in the domestic market until the launch of the face-lifted R170 in 2000. However, there were a few hidden changes, like a new crankshaft and con-rods for the M111 engine (added in time for the 1999 season), and minor revisions made to the cockpit floor lining (the main carpet) and the luggage box fitted to cars with the 'Tirefit' system. The lower seat cushion was also modified in the early part of 1999.

Meanwhile, the car was still evolving nicely in the States, with the 1999 Model Year machine now being offered in manual guise for $40,000 dead, while the automatic transmission became a $900 option. As well as the new map net just mentioned, the Brake Assist system and an automatic dimming rearview mirror were added to the spec list, while the more expensive of the two original mobile phone and CD-changer packages (the so-called K2 option), was the only one offered for 1999, although its price was reduced by $300 to $1595.

As well as being treated to some witty advertising, such as writing 'Sex Sells' in huge letters next to a silver car in one advert, and painting a yellow one with big red kisses in another, early 1999 also witnessed the issue of the first – and only, as it happens – Designo catalogue dedicated to the SLK.

The $3990 'Sport Package' was completely new for the US 1999 season, coming with 17-inch five-spoke alloy wheels (mounted with 225/45 ZR-rated rubber at the front and 245/40 tyres at the back), a front apron with integrated projector-beam foglights, side skirts, a rear valance, and special badging.

As if to prove there's no pleasing some people, having complained about the lack of a manual transmission and then got one, *Car & Driver* stated that it "was a step in the proper direction, but the gearbox was a clunky piece that made quick shifts impossible and didn't contribute significantly to making the SLK a more sporting car. So once again, in a 1999 sports car comparison, the sleek and comfy but bland-performing roadster finished last."

The cars for the 2000 season now had a $41,000 sticker price, but the small increase was easily covered by the addition of an automatic dimming facility on the driver's-side door mirror

Continued on page 129

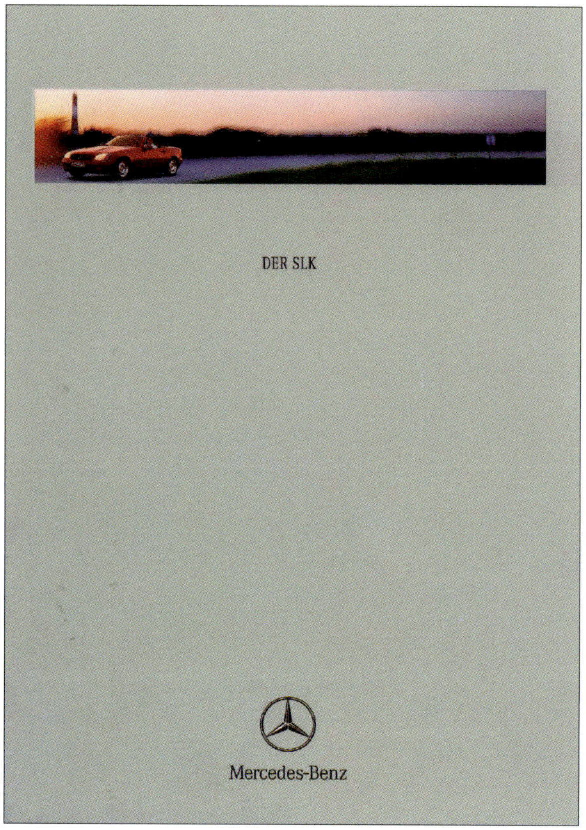

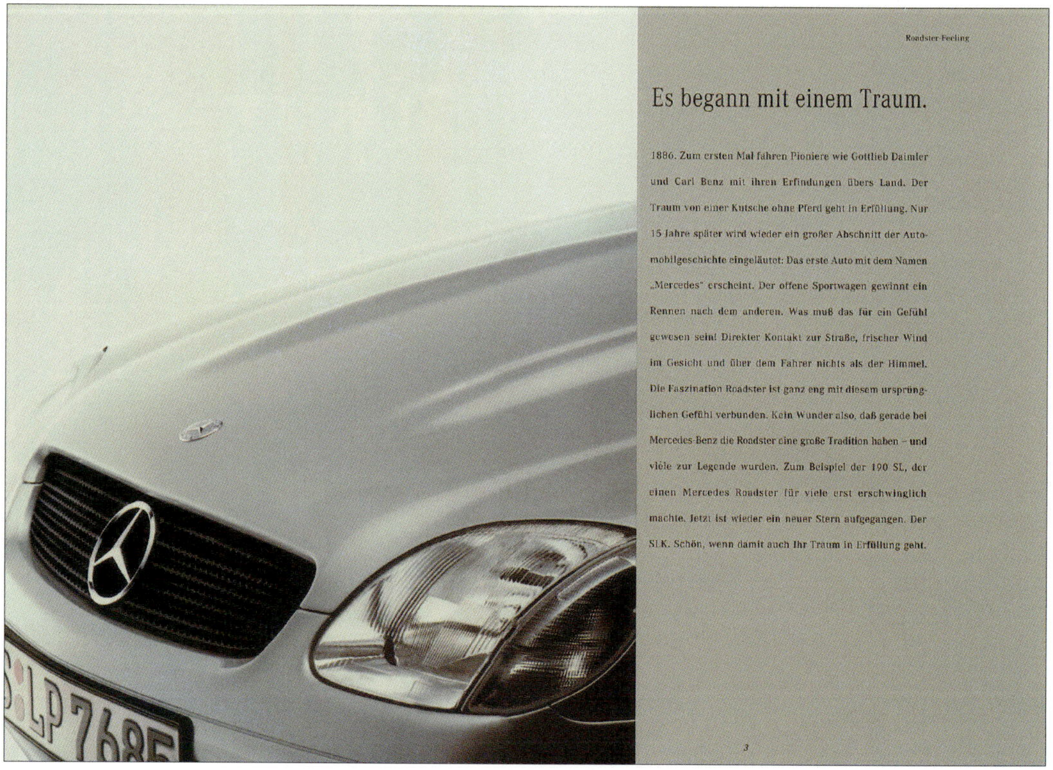

Selected pages from the 1999 German SLK catalogue.which was essentially the same as the original one printed in August 1996, suitably updated along the way to account for the minor changes in specification.

Auf den Long Island Expressway East, bis Exit 70.

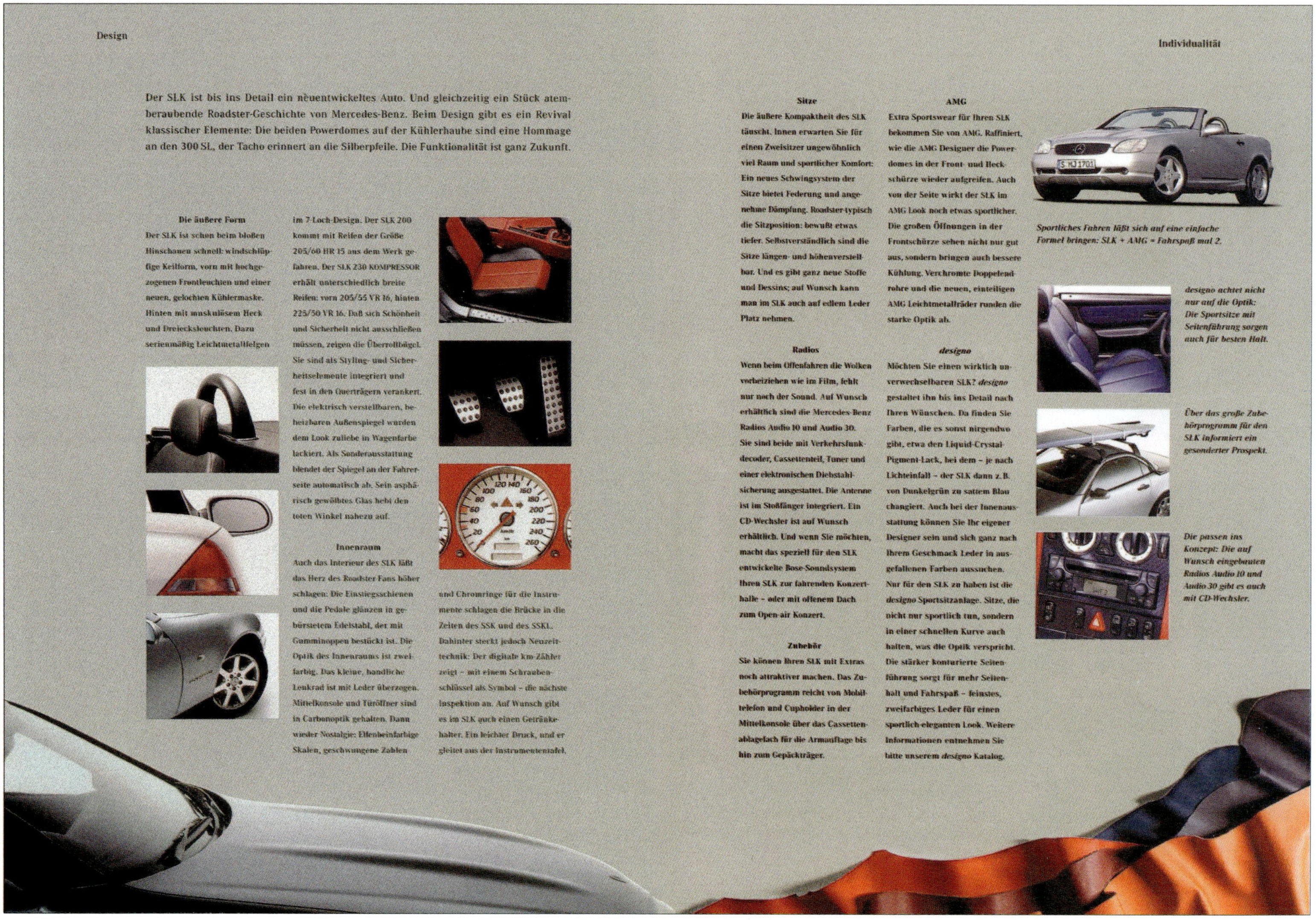

Design

Individualität

Der SLK ist bis ins Detail ein neuentwickeltes Auto. Und gleichzeitig ein Stück atemberaubende Roadster-Geschichte von Mercedes-Benz. Beim Design gibt es ein Revival klassischer Elemente: Die beiden Powerdomes auf der Kühlerhaube sind eine Hommage an den 300 SL, der Tacho erinnert an die Silberpfeile. Die Funktionalität ist ganz Zukunft.

Die äußere Form

Der SLK ist schon beim bloßen Hinschauen schnell: windschlüpfige Keilform, vorn mit hochgezogenen Frontleuchten und einer neuen, gelochten Kühlermaske. Hinten mit muskulösem Heck und Dreiecksleuchten. Dazu serienmäßig Leichtmetallfelgen im 7-Loch-Design. Der SLK 200 kommt mit Reifen der Größe 205/60 HR 15 aus dem Werk gefahren. Der SLK 230 KOMPRESSOR erhält unterschiedlich breite Reifen: vorn 205/55 VR 16, hinten 225/50 VR 16. Daß sich Schönheit und Sicherheit nicht ausschließen müssen, zeigen die Überrollbügel. Sie sind als Styling- und Sicherheitselemente integriert und fest in den Querträgern verankert. Die elektrisch verstellbaren, beheizbaren Außenspiegel wurden dem Look zuliebe in Wagenfarbe lackiert. Als Sonderausstattung blendet der Spiegel an der Fahrerseite automatisch ab. Sein asphärisch gewölbtes Glas hebt den toten Winkel nahezu auf.

Innenraum

Auch das Interieur des SLK läßt das Herz des Roadster-Fans höher schlagen: Die Einstiegsschienen und die Pedale glänzen in gebürstetem Edelstahl, der mit Gumminoppen bestückt ist. Die Optik des Innenraums ist zweifarbig. Das kleine, handliche Lenkrad ist mit Leder überzogen. Mittelkonsole und Türöffner sind in Carbonoptik gehalten. Dann wieder Nostalgie: Elfenbeinfarbige Skalen, geschwungene Zahlen und Chromringe für die Instrumente schlagen die Brücke in die Zeiten des SSK und des SSKL. Dahinter steckt jedoch Neuzeittechnik: Der digitale km-Zähler zeigt – mit einem Schraubenschlüssel als Symbol – die nächste Inspektion an. Auf Wunsch gibt es im SLK auch einen Getränkehalter. Ein leichter Druck, und er gleitet aus der Instrumententafel.

Sitze

Die äußere Kompaktheit des SLK täuscht. Innen erwarten Sie für einen Zweisitzer ungewöhnlich viel Raum und sportlicher Komfort: Ein neues Schwingsystem der Sitze bietet Federung und angenehme Dämpfung. Roadster-typisch die Sitzposition: bewußt etwas tiefer. Selbstverständlich sind die Sitze längen- und höhenverstellbar. Und es gibt ganz neue Stoffe und Dessins; auf Wunsch kann man im SLK auch auf edlem Leder Platz nehmen.

Radios

Wenn beim Offenfahren die Wolken vorbeiziehen wie im Film, fehlt nur noch der Sound. Auf Wunsch erhältlich sind die Mercedes-Benz Radios Audio 10 und Audio 30. Sie sind beide mit Verkehrsfunkdecoder, Cassettenteil, Tuner und einer elektronischen Diebstahlsicherung ausgestattet. Die Antenne ist im Stoßfänger integriert. Ein CD-Wechsler ist auf Wunsch erhältlich. Und wenn Sie möchten, macht das speziell für den SLK entwickelte Bose-Soundsystem Ihren SLK zur fahrenden Konzerthalle – oder mit offenem Dach zum Open-air Konzert.

Zubehör

Sie können Ihren SLK mit Extras noch attraktiver machen. Das Zubehörprogramm reicht von Mobiltelefon und Cupholder in der Mittelkonsole über das Cassettenablagefach für die Armauflage bis hin zum Gepäckträger.

AMG

Extra Sportswear für Ihren SLK bekommen Sie von AMG. Raffiniert, wie die AMG Designer die Powerdomes in der Front- und Heckschürze wieder aufgreifen. Auch von der Seite wirkt der SLK im AMG Look noch etwas sportlicher. Die großen Öffnungen in der Frontschürze sehen nicht nur gut aus, sondern bringen auch bessere Kühlung. Verchromte Doppelendrohre und die neuen, einteiligen AMG Leichtmetallräder runden die starke Optik ab.

designo

Möchten Sie einen wirklich unverwechselbaren SLK? *designo* gestaltet ihn bis ins Detail nach Ihren Wünschen. Da finden Sie Farben, die es sonst nirgendwo gibt, etwa den Liquid-Crystal-Pigment-Lack, bei dem – je nach Lichteinfall – der SLK dann z. B. von Dunkelgrün zu sattem Blau changiert. Auch bei der Innenausstattung können Sie Ihr eigener Designer sein und sich ganz nach Ihrem Geschmack Leder in ausgefallenen Farben aussuchen. Nur für den SLK zu haben ist die *designo* Sportsitzanlage. Sitze, die nicht nur sportlich tun, sondern in einer schnellen Kurve auch halten, was die Optik verspricht. Die stärker konturierte Seitenführung sorgt für mehr Seitenhalt und Fahrspaß – feinstes, zweifarbiges Leder für einen sportlich-eleganten Look. Weitere Informationen entnehmen Sie bitte unserem *designo* Katalog.

Sportliches Fahren läßt sich auf eine einfache Formel bringen: SLK + AMG = Fahrspaß mal 2.

designo achtet nicht nur auf die Optik: Die Sportsitze mit Seitenführung sorgen auch für besten Halt.

Über das große Zubehörprogramm für den SLK informiert ein gesonderter Prospekt.

Die passen ins Konzept: Die auf Wunsch eingebauten Radios Audio 10 und Audio 30 gibt es auch mit CD-Wechsler.

THE AMG STORY

The Mercedes brand has always managed to attract the attentions of tuning companies, but few are as synonymous with the Stuttgart maker as AMG of Burgstall, Baden-Württemberg, and later Affalterbach, a few miles to the north-east of Stuttgart.

AMG was officially founded in June 1967 by Hans-Werner Aufrecht (who'd worked for Daimler-Benz, and had been in the competition department building engines in the glory days of the 1950s) and Erhard Melcher. For the first ten years of its history, AMG concentrated on engine and suspension development to further its highly-successful racing programme, but body kits and wheels were added to the firm's catalogue, and, ultimately, complete cars were built and offered for sale, either in turnkey guise or to the specific requests of customers.

In 1983, AMG developed a four-valve per cylinder head for the V8, leading to signature vehicles like the Hammer, but it also provided the foundation stone for further expansion, not just in Germany, but in places as far afield as America and Japan. The bored-out, 6-litre 32v conversion on the 5-litre V8, around since 1987, would duly provide enthusiasts with the 500SL 6.0 AMG.

The real breakthrough, however, came in October 1990, when AMG secured a deal in which its tuning parts could be sold and fitted via Mercedes-Benz dealerships, and complete cars started filtering through into domestic showrooms by May 1991. In addition, the racing programme was treated as a partnership, with the works DTM cars being prepared by Aufrecht's company. On the 1st January 1999, DaimlerChrysler bought a 51 per cent stake in AMG, sealing the relationship once and for all with the foundation of Mercedes-AMG GmbH.

Japanese advertising from the summer of 1997. This piece features the AMG bodykit and wheels that were available as an option for the SLK in most countries.

and heated screen washer nozzles. Most options increased in price also. Although the automatic transmission continued unchanged, metallic paint and heated front seats went up by $10, the 'Sport Package' by $60, and the K2 option up by $200 due to the former analogue phone being replaced by a digital Motorola unit.

Also new for 2000 was a pair of Designo SLK packages. The 'Electric Green Edition' came with metallic paint in that colour, and charcoal Nappa leather on the seats, steering wheel, console, roll bars and floormat piping, adding a $4250 premium to the car's basic price, which had to be ordered with heated seats. The latter was also a requirement on the Designo 'Copper Edition' (with special paint, and copper/charcoal Nappa leather on the same areas as those described against the other Designo model), which added $4700 to the invoice.

America signed off with a 'Limited Edition' introduced in December 1999, featuring Obsidian Black paintwork, polished 17-inch EVO II six-spoke alloy wheels, an Oyster/Charcoal leather interior, a CD-changer and phone, special badging and floormats, and a stainless exhaust tip.

Japanese Castrol advertising from 1999, using the SLK to try and put some romance back into motoring.

As for the other key export markets, in Britain, there was a small price increase applied to the SLK in January 1999, taking the SLK230 Kompressor (AT only, and the only grade available in the UK) up to £31,640. This was the first time the price had gone up on the two-seater, but it then stayed the same for another year, until the face-lifted car came along. Nothing happened in the Japanese market whatsoever, with pricing and the single model policy carried over from the time of the SLK's introduction. As for Australia, the 1999 MY SLK200 was listed at $88,100, while the SLK230 Kompressor commanded an extra $11,300. These prices then stayed the same going into the summer of 2000, when they were reduced a fraction to clear the last of the old cars before the new ones arrived.

Meanwhile, the Vision SLR coupé concept had been presented at the 1999 Detroit Show, the 5.4 litre supercharged machine suitably impressing the crowds gathered before it. A couple of months later, in Geneva, the new CL-Class (C215) was unveiled, along with the CLK 55 AMG. As it happens, a whole new range of AMG machines was launched in April 1999, with the SL 73 AMG being considered the flagship of the line.

A face-lifted E-Class (W210) was presented in July 1999, with the CLK updated in the following month. All CLK, SL and C-Class models came with the Electronic Stability Programme (ESP) as standard from now – something that would also be adopted on the SLK in the very near future. The relentless pace of development

The Vision SLR, seen here in roadster guise at the 1999 Tokyo Show. This concept model revealed a number of future Mercedes styling cues, pointing the way forward.

continued with a roadster version of the V8-powered Vision SLR being displayed at the 1999 Frankfurt Show. New engines were announced for the S-Class at the same time, making the most of the latest in diesel technology, and before the year came to an end, the AMG range expanded once more, just after the celebrations surrounding Mercedes-Benz winning another F1 driver's title with Mika Hakkinen were starting to die down.

Another cause for celebration came at the start of the year 2000, when the Stuttgart company decided to launch its face-lifted version of the R170. Regarding the 170,719 early cars, of the 44,846 SLK200s built, 13,928 were equipped with an automatic transmission, and no less than 85,321 of the 113,520 SLK230 Kompressor models built had the 5AT unit. The rare SLK200 Kompressor accounted for another 12,353 SLK sales, although this particular model was only ever offered with a manual gearbox.

The 'Silver Arrows' legend was kept alive in the FIA GT Championships and the Grand Prix arena. This is the Mercedes-Benz that won the 1999 F1 title for Mika Hakkinen. The German manufacturer had won both the constructor's and driver's titles in the previous year, helping to enhance the company's sporting profile.

4

THE R170 FACE-LIFT

"There were plenty of reasons to like the Mercedes-Benz SLK230 Kompressor when it debuted in 1997, but hard-driving pleasure was not one of them. When it comes to roadsters, we're a bunch that values invigorating driving above all else ... For 2001, the SLK gets two new additions that should help it become more of an enthusiast's car: a 3.2-litre V6 engine providing 25 more ponies than the supercharged four, and a six-speed manual gearbox." – *Car & Driver*, June 2000.

The Mercedes Vision SLA concept car put in an appearance at the 2000 Detroit Show – a small, open two-seater based on the A-Class, but featuring a number of styling cues that pointed towards the future of the SLK. Using an aluminium body to reduce weight, the 950kg (2090lb) SLA was an interesting idea in an age when each model generation increased in size, and engines became ever more powerful to cope with the extra bulk. With thoughts slowly but surely turning to ecology matters, it was probably cost that held back the project, for lightweight aluminium is far more expensive than steel, and for an entry-level machine, keeping the sticker price low is an important factor.

Even though the 1.9-litre Vision SLA hogged the limelight, it seems rather ironic in that respect that the Detroit Show, which opened on 15 January, was used in conjunction with the Brussels Show in Europe (held at roughly the same time) to announce the face-lifted version of the R170 SLK, complete with a larger V6 engine!

Jorg Prigl, the SLK's project leader in the early days, had said back in 1996: "At the moment, there are no plans for a six-cylinder version [of the SLK]. We don't think our customers will ask for a six, once they have driven the Kompressor."

In reality, with the SLK selling like hotcakes, sight unseen, why would the Mercedes people say there was an even more impressive model in the pipeline? The lack of a six also provided the marketing folks with a useful angle from which to distance the cheaper car from the SL, which was doubtless far more profitable for the Stuttgart company. Only when the honeymoon sales period was over did rumours of the six-cylinder SLK begin flying again, and with the competition offering sixes from an early stage in model development, augmenting the SLK line-up with a larger, smoother engine was an entirely logical move.

New drivetrains

It was no coincidence that the SLK's engine bay had been designed to accept a six-cylinder engine from the off, but it's configuration was that of a compact vee rather than a traditional straight-six, as the latter would have upset the car's handling and crash deformation control, as well as making it longer.

The M112 90-degree V6s, introduced to the SL line in the spring of 1998, came with all-aluminium alloy construction (rather than the alloy head and cast iron block arrangement of the straight-sixes), saving a significant amount of weight. In a world first, even the cylinder liners were made of light alloy with a high silicon content, allowing a good compromise between reducing weight and friction whilst maintaining long-term service and reliability levels.

The M112 units were unusual in having three valves per cylinder instead of four (a single exhaust valve to one side of the combustion chamber, with two smaller inlet valves on the other),

The Vision SLA concept which appeared at the 2000 Detroit Show.

their operation designed in such a way as to allow the use of a single overhead camshaft per bank. From a technical standpoint, the single exhaust valve reduced heat loss in the exhaust gases, thus making the catalytic converter heat up quicker and work in its most efficient operating band more of the time.

Another interesting feature was the dual ignition, with two coils and two sparkplugs per cylinder, the plugs located in a line directly between the exhaust valve and pair of inlet valves, and one plug to each side of them on the outside. All told, with an electric air pump added into the equation, the new specification promised a ten per cent fuel saving, faster warm-up times, and significantly lower emission values.

To enhance engine flexibility, the microprocessor-controlled sequential port fuel-injection took advantage of variable length intake manifold technology, with the manifold structure cast in magnesium alloy as part of the weight-saving programme. Indeed, the intelligent selection of lightweight materials throughout the 18v powerplant made the new V6s 25 per cent lighter than their straight-six equivalent, while a balance shaft was something new for the V6, reducing first and second order vibration.

Display version of an M112 V6 from the time, the cutaway sections clearly showing its internal workings, along with those of the automatic transmission tacked onto the back.

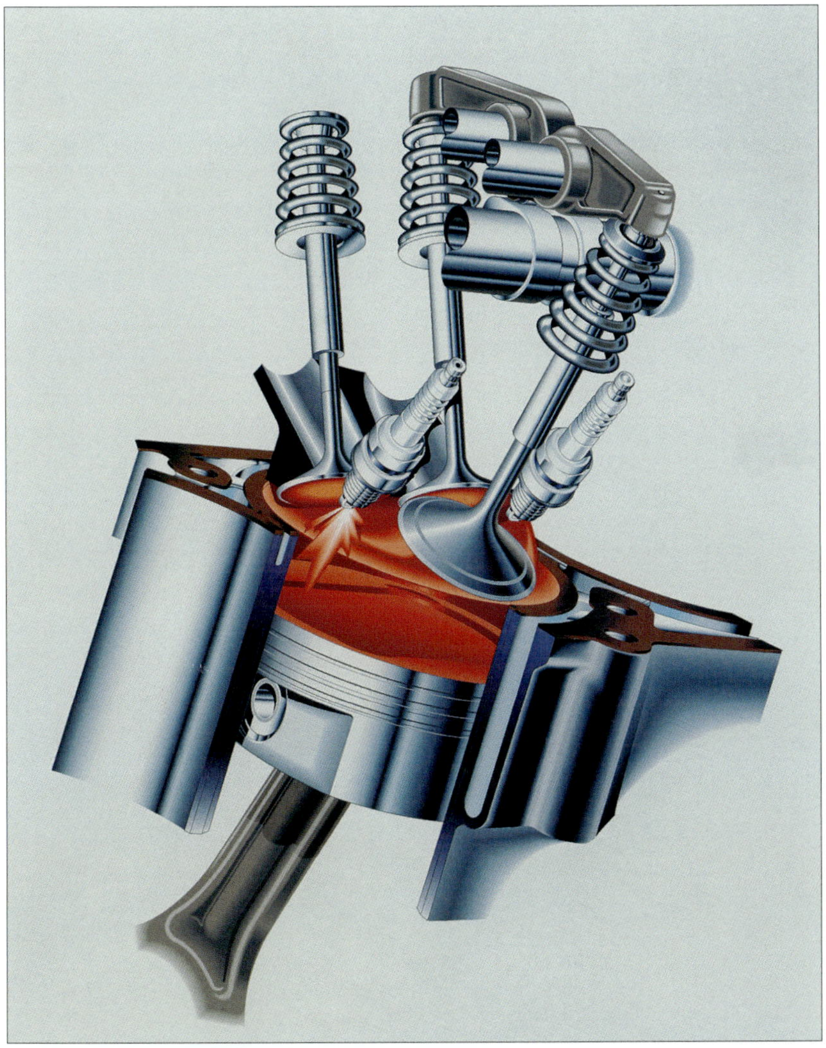

The unusual three-valve per cylinder arrangement of the M112 engine, with two inlets and a single exhaust valve. Note also the two sparkplugs for each cylinder, and their location.

Interestingly, although a 2.8- and a 3.2-litre version of the M112 were listed for the R129 SL, the supercharged engine used in the SLK delivered similar performance levels to the smaller V6, so only the M112 E32 3199cc powerplant was offered. Designated the Type 112.947 (the 112.943 was used in the SL), it had a four-bearing bottom-end, an 89.9mm x 84.0mm bore and stroke measurement, a Bosch ME 2.8 black box hooked up to a hot film air mass sensor (HFM), and a 10.0:1 compression ratio, all combining to give 218bhp, along with 229lbft of torque.

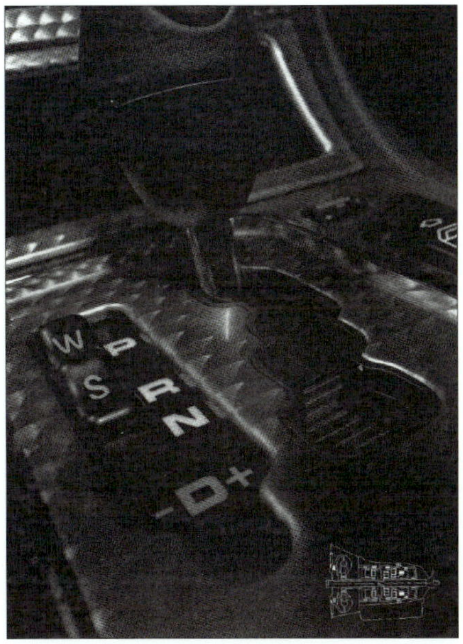

Detail shot of the 'Touchshift' selector on the latest automatic transmissions, introduced on the SLK line as part of the 2000 face-lift.

The V6 was given a five-speed automatic transmission – much the same as the earlier version internally, carrying the same W5A330 designation, and continuing with the same ratios. As such, it came with 3.93 on first, 2.41 on second, 1.49 on third, a direct fourth, and an overdriven 0.83 fifth. The final-drive was unchanged, too, listed at 3.27:1. There was one major difference, though, and that was in the selector gate design. All face-lifted cars came with 'Touchshift' – a facility that allowed the driver to nudge the gearlever to the left when in 'D' for downshifts, and to the right to execute an upshift. The traditional staggered gate was therefore abandoned beyond the 'P', 'R' and 'N' positions, and an LED gear indicator window was added to the left of the clock. For the record, the gearbox's code number was 722.618 when matched up to the V6 machine.

The manual transmission was completely different to the earlier version, being a six-speed unit built by Daimler AG at its Gaggenau plant. The V6 car was equipped with the SG-S400/5.3 model (code 716.660 or 716.667), with cogs giving 4.46, 2.61, 1.72, 1.25, 1.00 and 0.84, while the 3.27:1 final-drive was carried over. The selector had four planes, with reverse down and to the left, then first through sixth being arranged in a double-H pattern off to the right of the reverse plane.

The six-speed manual gearbox made a huge difference to the SLK's sporting potential. Note the shift pattern, and the regular gearknob and gaiter.

The SLK200 Kompressor was continued, but was now powered by the M111 E20 EVO ML (Type 111.958) unit, which had a Siemens SIM 4 LE engine management system, a modified cylinder head with better combustion properties, a revised supercharger, which was both quieter and lighter thanks to the removal of its electromagnetic clutch, and a more efficient exhaust manifold. However, despite a higher compression ratio, raised from 8.5:1 to 9.5:1, this didn't stop power output falling to 163bhp/170lbft, showing just how strict EU emission regulations were becoming. Previously limited to just a handful of countries, from 2000, with the 2-litre NA grade discontinued, the SLK200 Kompressor was now the entry-level machine in most markets.

Following the face-lift, the SLK200 Kompressor was at last given an automatic transmission option, inheriting the W5A330 unit used earlier on the original strict SLK200 and SLK230 Kompressor models, albeit with a different 722.616 code number to define the 'Touchshift' version now in use, and a different 3.46:1 final-drive ratio – taller than that specified for the old NA car, but lower than that of the first 2.3-litre supercharged machine. The internal ratios were the same as those listed against the new six-cylinder car.

Equally important was the adoption of the six-speed manual, the 2-litre supercharged model coming with the SG-S270/5.3 version (code 716.622 or 716.630), although the internal ratios were the same as those found in the SG-S400 gearbox, while the final drive was the same 3.46:1 one as the automatic car.

A few changes were applied to the SLK230 Kompressor model's engine, too, bringing forth a new type number (111.983) and M111 M23 EVO ML designation. The Bosch engine management system was changed to a Siemens SIM 4 LE version, with a hot film air mass sensor HFM and individual ignition coils (two had been employed for the four plugs before). After all these modifications, along with the refined cylinder head, blower and exhaust manifold designs found on the other M111 lump, the 2295cc unit delivered 197bhp (an increase of 4bhp over the earlier version, albeit 200rpm further up the rev-range), and the

The 2-litre supercharged engine (Type 111.958), which delivered 163bhp at 5300rpm, along with 170lbft of torque at between 2500 and 4800rpm.

A useful picture, as it shows the cruise control wand with its limiter feature, as well as the 'LIM' light burning bright in the centre of the speedometer. It also shows the gear indicator added to the left of the clock in the base of the tachometer.

same 207lbft of torque as before. Interestingly, there was also enhanced fuel economy, amounting to around a four per cent saving overall.

As it happens, both the 5AT and 6MT gearboxes were exactly the same as those specified for the SLK200 Kompressor model, even down to the code numbers. This naturally meant the internal ratios were the same, although the bigger-engined car was given a 3.27:1 back axle, matching that of the V6 model. Surprisingly, all SLKs from now on, whether manual or automatic, came with cruise control as standard, and those sold in Europe had the 'Speedtronic' limiter as an added feature, with a 'LIM' light directly underneath the speedometer's centre spindle showing when it was in operation.

On the 'green' side of things, it's worth noting that all the face-lifted SLKs complied with EURO 4 emissions standards, not due to take effect until January 2005, and had a 'check engine' lamp tied into the car's onboard diagnostics (OBD), added to the left-hand bank of warning lights to alert the driver that a system relating to emission control wasn't functioning properly. This could include the ECU and injection setup, the exhaust, or even a loose fuel cap. In addition, all cars, regardless of whether they had air-conditioning or not, gained an electric cooling fan at this stage, reducing unnecessary load on the engine, which naturally helps save fuel, and those shipped to Canada and the like were fitted with a cylinder block preheater to speed along warm-up times and thus reduce emissions that way.

The face-lifted front-end (left), with a revised bumper section and lower apron. This is a four-cylinder car, by the way, which had a different lower air intake profile to the V6 model, while the wheels (SA code 648) are the ones that came as standard on the SLK230 Kompressor. The 'Kompressor' badge, incidentally, was carried over from the earlier supercharged machines.The front of a V6 model is pictured right, with its unique lower section to the front bumper assembly. Note also the standard headlights, the headlight washers, and the larger brakes peeking out from behind the five-spoke alloys that came as part of the SLK320 package.

Other changes

To go with the latest powerplants and revised transmission options, the body was given a minor face-lift as well. Starting at the front, a new bumper assembly was grafted onto the shell, with the inserts now fatter at the outer edges to give an angled look to the grille surround. With the benefit of a side view, one can see the bumper was actually a fraction bigger, front to back, adding 15mm (0.6in) to the length of the car.

The grille itself, whilst basically unchanged, was finished in a lighter colour to make it stand out more, and below the number plate, the air intake was simplified (particularly so in the case of the four-cylinders cars) and oval-shaped foglights were adopted, while the lowest section of the apron was more shapely and finished in body colour. Careful inspection revealed another bib spoiler further underneath the car, blacked out so as to hide it from view, and the headlight washer covers (when fitted) were given softer profiles. On the subject of headlights, Xenon headlights were listed as a new option for all cars in most markets.

Moving further back, there were new alloy wheel designs for the more expensive grades (the SLK200 Kompressor continued with the old 15-inch SLK200 rims, the SLK230 Kompressor had new 16-inch six-spoke wheels, while the SLK320 came with a five-spoke version), and the repeater indicator on the side of the front wings was deleted. A fresh door mirror design was employed, incorporating the indicator removed from the wing,

The latest door mirrors, incorporating the repeater indicators previously mounted on the trailing edge of the front wings.

A useful shot showing the subtly redesigned rear combination lamps, as well as the luggage compartment, which was surprisingly big when the top was up. Note also the first aid kit and warning triangle, along with the stubby telephone mast on the nearside rear wing. The radio aerial continued to be hidden under the bumper on European cars.

while the door handles were colour-keyed in one of the ten regular paint shades now on offer. The sill panels were also finished in body colour, and similar in shape to those seen on the Turin and Paris Show cars of 1994 vintage. Visually, the car was a lot less delicate-looking as a result, which tended to fit in with the beefier engine options and the sportier image the marketing people were aspiring to.

Around the back, the rear light clusters looked the same, but had softer edges on the clear sections, while the bumper blade was given a full-width insert and finished completely in body colour, visually giving the car a lot of extra volume, as well as a more solid appearance. The lower corners were also far more shapely, adding aerodynamic efficiency, and the guard on the trailing edge of the wheelarch was a touch heavier. Other details to look out for included oval-shaped exhaust pipes, and the end of the boot lock – it now being hidden underneath the boot plinth, between the nearside number plate light and the boot release handle. It was hardly the most useful of positions, but in reality, it was very rarely used.

This was certainly a comprehensive face-lift, as there were a number of changes under the skin, too, with further strengthening in the front bulkhead, floorpan and side members to enhance the car's rigidity and crashworthiness. The door shells were also modified to disperse crash energy into the stronger B-posts and the panelling just aft of it, while modifications to the engine bay in the area of the brake master cylinder reduced the risk of the pedal set injuring the driver. There was also an enlarged fuel tank – it's capacity upped from 53 litres (11.6 Imperial, or 14.0 US gallons) to 60 litres (13.2 Imperial, or 15.9 US gallons), extending the car's range by a useful amount.

A side view of the face-lifted SLK, giving a much better look at the revised aerodynamics package. The new cars were much heavier than their predecessors, with the SLK230 Kompressor gaining 60kg (132lb) after the face-lift, for instance. Even the 2-litre machine tipped the scales at 1365kg (3009lb), while the V6 model seen here had a 1405kg (3097lb) kerb weight.

This angle gives us a good, clear view of the face-lifted tail, complete with the oval-shaped stainless exhaust trim. The styling looked a lot less fussy with the boot lock hidden out of sight.

The inside story

On opening the door, one was greeted to an array of new sights. The SLK certainly went upmarket in a hurry, basically becoming a compact SL during the face-lift, which perhaps points to the SLA being a greater possibility for production than we'd at first expected, although over a decade down the line, it still has yet to appear. For sure, the SLK's rivals had all matured, each becoming more luxurious or at the very least more refined with every passing sales season.

Although the interior's basic layout and the shapes of the major components were all instantly recognizable, the overriding impression from within the cockpit had changed from youthful and sporty to luxurious, with a hint of sportiness. Material selection had a lot to do with this change in moods,

Interior of a face-lifted SLK200 Kompressor. Note the aluminium trim pieces on the centre console and doors, the latest steering wheel and treadplate designs, and also the interior light on the header rail, this being a new version which incorporated a hands-free microphone and intruder sensor (to go with option 882), as well as the TeleAid button – marked 'SOS' when fitted, but blanked off in this picture. The optional transmitter for the garage opener was fitted between the interior light housing and rearview mirror, when specified.

The stylish interior of an automatic SLK320 with 'Calyptus Linea' wood trim.

The colour of the gauge faces was changed to a shade called 'Mussel' during the face-lift. Note the 6200rpm red-line, 100rpm higher than that on the V6 cars.

with new 'Arezzo' cloth and fresh leather shades, as well as different seat trim that looked more inviting, moving away from the pure bucket shell concept (or at least making it less obvious), the end of the carbonfibre-style facing pieces, and a simpler approach to things like the steering wheel design.

While the two-tone theme was carried over, the quickest way to sum up the interior transformation is in the replacement of the carbon-type trim pieces for engine-turned aluminium ones on the centre console and door handle surrounds, with the lighting switch and air vent escutcheon panels now having a plain black finish. As an option, though, the aluminium sections could be replaced by one of two shades of wood trim for those looking for a more luxurious atmosphere.

Detailing included the adoption of narrower spokes on the steering wheel (still 380mm/15in in diameter), with the horn push moved to the centre boss, and only the inner top edge of the rim taking up the two-tone concept. On wheels with wood trim, the same section gained 'Calyptus Linea', blackened 'Bird's Eye Maple' or Designo wood, along with two matching pieces added at the four o'clock and eight o'clock positions. The gearlever was also trimmed to match, varying between interior colour choices.

Gauge faces went from an 'Ivory' to 'Mussel' shade at the same time, and a chrome release button was employed on the handbrake, rather than a black plastic one. Power seats were a new option, with the controls on the chairs themselves in the form of a mini-seat, as had become traditional at Mercedes, although the headrest adjustment remained manual nonetheless, and all buyers benefited from more support in the seats. One should also be aware of the new treadplate design, with an 'SLK' insignia on four-cylinder cars, and a 'V6' one on the SLK320 model.

Rounding things off

On the chassis front, the suspension was stiffened up and lowered by 5mm (0.2in), gaining a rear anti-roll bar along the way, and the Electronic Stability Programme (ESP), first introduced in the early part of 1994, was made standard across the SLK line. This replaced the ASR traction control system used previously, although it built on the latter's hardware, using the ABS sensors to determine the onset of oversteer or understeer, and selectively reducing engine torque or applying one of the rear brakes to bring the car back into control. For enthusiastic drivers, it was possible to cancel ESP via a rocker switch mounted in the bank of switches below the radio. Finally, to keep the additional performance in check, the V6 model was given larger front brakes. These measured 300mm (11.8in) across, 12mm (0.5in) greater than the disc diameter found on the four-cylinder models, although all cars shared the same rear brake setup.

Having established what made up the face-lift, the next chapter looks at the individual major markets, and then takes the story through to the end of the R170 run.

The button allowing the ESP system to be turned off can be seen next to the hazard warning light switch. One can also see the drilled pedal set, along with the small luggage net introduced in 1998 off to the right.

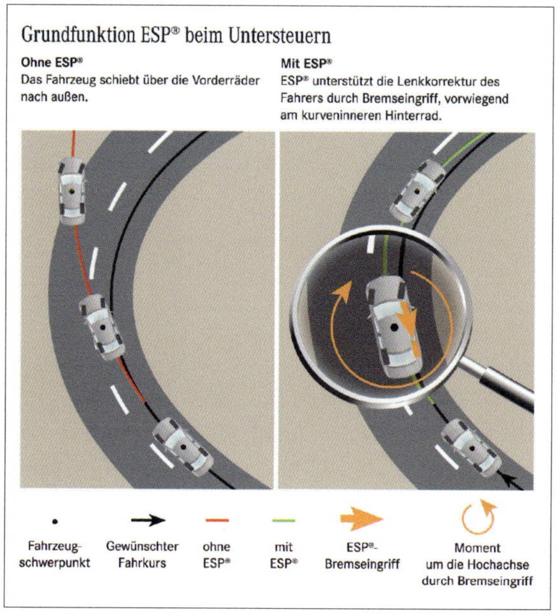

Press material explaining the ESP principle.

The following pages show selected spreads from the first domestic catalogue, printed in February 2000.

Jeder Tag ist ein Geschenk.

Inhalt:

Tradition	*2*
Ansichten	*4*
Der SLK im Detail	*14*
Technik	*22*
Antrieb	*24*
Sicherheit	*26*
Individualität	*28*
Dienstleistungen	*30*
Ausstattung	*32*
Technische Daten	*34*
Lacke und Polster	*36*

Hier geht selbst die Sonne auf, wenn sie mal nicht scheint.

Beim SLK fängt das Tempo bereits bei 0 an.
Aus dem Stand beschleunigt er den Puls.

5

END OF THE LINE

"With its sporty, elegant styling and trick power-convertible hardtop, the Mercedes-Benz SLK230 Kompressor has never had trouble attracting positive attention. Where it falls off the enthusiasm curve is in the power department. The original supercharged in-line four-cylinder engine just didn't deliver the satisfyingly quick output the sporty lines seem to promise. For 2001, that problem is solved." – *Motor Trend,* July 2000.

Two pieces of German advertising, taken from a series promoting the SLK produced in 2000.

It was fascinating to see how quickly the SLK had come of age – a rebellious youth brought into line to more closely resemble a vehicle expected of its ancestry. It's also interesting to note that the SL was sequentially becoming ever more sporting, but with the flagship of the range costing almost exactly four times the asking price of an SLK230 Kompressor in its native Germany, the two drophead models were effectively kept well apart from each other in the showrooms.

The domestic market

Without taxes (VAT was 16 per cent in Germany at the time), the face-lifted SLK200 Kompressor was priced at DM 51,800 at the start of 2000, while the SLK230 Kompressor commanded DM 56,900, and the SLK320 a cool DM 66,900 in manual guise. Standard equipment and options were pretty much carried over if we use equivalent model lines, although it's worth doing a recap here, seeing as we're entering a new chapter and a new phase in the development of the R170 series.

This is a domestic SLK200 Kompressor model, but looks just like a 2.3-litre car from the front and side, as it has the latter's alloy wheels (bought via option code 648).

Standard features on home market models included alloy wheels, a six-speed manual transmission with a clutch-starter interlock, cruise control and speed limiter functions, the ESP stability programme, anti-lock brakes with Brake Assist, power-assisted steering (PAS), the 'Tirefit' system (with an electric compressor and a can of sealant rather than a spare wheel), power-adjusted and heated door mirrors, front and rear foglights, power windows with green-tinted glass all-round, a heated rear screen with timer, remote central locking with immobilizer and panic switch, cloth trim, sports seats with height adjustment and adjustable headrests on both sides, stainless treadplates, dual front and side airbags,

Continued on page 154

Various views of a German-registered SLK320 with its top down. These are the standard alloy wheels for this model.

The tasteful interior of an SLK320 built for the European mainland, this car featuring an automatic transmission and the 'Calyptus Linea' wood trim, which looked particularly luxurious. The small tray in the dashboard top roll could be replaced by a cupholder insert as a no-cost option.

Studio shot of a domestic SLK320 with its top up.

individual heater controls, full instrumentation including an 'Assyst' service reminder feature, an outside temperature gauge, digital clock, a lights-on and handbrake warning chime, soft storage pockets in the doors and on the rear bulkhead, audio preparation, a hazard warning triangle, first aid kit, a windblocker, and a locking luggage box in the boot.

Regarding the alloy wheels, the SLK200 Kompressor left the factory with the old 15-inch wheel and tyre combination. The SLK230 Kompressor and SLK320 ran on 16-inch rims – the 7J fronts being mounted with 205/55 VR-rated rubber, while the 8J rears had 225/50 tyres fitted. Alternatively, 17-inch alloys were an option, both in regular seven-spoke Mercedes and five-spoke

Xenon headlights were a new option for the face-lifted cars (SA code 612).

AMG designs, but we will come to these in a minute. The only other difference on the spec list was standard air-conditioning for the SLK320 model, which now came complete with a 'REST' switch, allowing the engine's residual heat to keep the cockpit warm without the motor running.

Regular options included an automatic transmission with cruise control and the 'Speedtronic' limiter (SA code 423, priced at DM 3200), the AMG bodykit (772) at DM 6950, metallic paint at DM 950 (Designo metallic paint was also available at DM 2600, while Designo Varicolor shades were listed as a DM 4000 extra), self-reacting anti-dazzle mirrors (249) at DM 500 for all three, a heated windscreen washer system (875) at DM 300, Xenon headlights (612) at DM 1600, headlight washers (600) at DM 450, an uprated battery (673) at DM 105, steering column adjustment (441) at DM 260, air-conditioning (580) at DM 2300, an alarm system (551), which was DM 510, or DM 820 if upgraded with interior protection (882), a garage door opener (231) at DM 350, cassette holder (331) or CD holder (330), both priced at DM 85, a fire extinguisher (682) at DM 190, seat heaters (873) at DM 560, power seat adjustment (560) at DM 1500, and a luggage rack (726) at DM 100. No-cost options (NCO) included a spacesaver spare (SA code 669, replacing the 'Tirefit' system and luggage box), and a cupholder insert (309) in place of the oddments tray in the dashboard top roll.

Leather trim was still available, priced at DM 1800 (or DM 3950 if Designo leather was selected), with wood trim a new option: the black 'Bird's-Eye Maple' (SA code 732) suiting all interior choices, but the walnut-like 'Calyptus Linea' wood (734) not being recommended with blue, red or yellow upholstery. Both wood trim sets were listed at DM 1000, but there were also Designo options, including a Designo wood/leather steering wheel (Y95) at DM 1430, a Designo wood and leather gearlever (Y94) at DM 365, Designo wood trim accents on the console and door handle finishing plates at DM 1000, Designo leather on the centre console (Y97) at DM 1170, and Designo leather on the roll-over hoops (Y98) at DM 1070.

The 16-inch alloys fitted to the SLK230 Kompressor as standard (SA code 648), were priced at DM 820 if specified on the 2-litre car, while the SLK320 alloy wheels (688) were DM 1130 extra, or DM 310 on the 2.3-litre machine, as that was already running with 16-inch rims. The 17-inch wheel and tyre combination (689) cost between DM 1150 and DM 2280 depending on the car it was to be fitted to, while the AMG option (794), added between DM 2220 and DM 3350 to the invoice. All-weather tyres (645) were a NCO on 16-inch wheels, or DM 205 extra if specified on 15-inch rims.

On the audio and communication front, there was the Mercedes-Benz Audio 10 unit (753), which was DM 800, or DM 980 in CD guise (SA code 756). The Mercedes-Benz Audio 30 (750) was DM 1480, although an APS navigation system could be integrated into the CD-based unit (353) for DM 1920 extra. Buying four speakers without a radio (SA code 533) cost DM 330, while upgrading to a Bose sound system (810) commanded DM 950. As for the telephones, there was a 'Handy' unit (317), or a 'Standard' phone (316), both of which were about DM 1500 plus fitting, while a tail-mounted antenna (270) was DM 150 extra.

Another price list was issued in April 2000, although, as one would expect, it was almost identical to the one printed in January. The only differences were the addition of Designo Mystic paint at DM 4000, Designo Chromaflair paint at DM 8600, and

The Mercedes-Benz stand at the 2000 Geneva Show, an SLK flanked by a convertible version of the CLK on one side, and an R129 SL on the other.

new telephones – the 317 unit being replaced by a 854 version, while the 316 model was superseded by the 853 option.

Meanwhile, on the corporate front, Bob Eaton retired in March 2000, just as the new W203 C-Class was being launched. Dieter Zetsche and Wolfgang Bernhard were sent from Stuttgart to the US to hold the fort, as what amounted to a take-over rather than a merger emerged. A little while later, as the empire building continued on Schrempp's watch, DaimlerChrysler took a one-third stake in Japan's Mitsubishi Motors in July 2000.

The new car in America

Sales of the face-lifted car began in the States just a few weeks after the Detroit Show closed its doors, with the car officially classed as an early 2001 model in the US. The V6-engined SLK320 joining the line-up was naturally the biggest news for fans of the two-seater, priced at $43,900 – $5000 more than the face-lifted 2.3-litre supercharged car, which was actually cheaper than before. As such, the two newcomers sat either side of the old model's $41,000 price line.

Things were simplified somewhat for American buyers, with the four-cylinder machine coming with aluminium trim pieces on the centre console and door handle surrounds, while the six-cylinder car had wood trim as standard, extending to the steering wheel and gearshift. All SLKs came with leather trim, air-conditioning, remote central locking, a Bose sound system, Tele Aid with GPS tracking, and, of course, things like ESP, which had been made standard in Europe since the face-lift. Wheels were the same as those found on home market machines, meaning the SLK320 had different 16-inch rims to the 2.3-litre car, and also sported power seats and steering column adjustment – the latter previously part of the SLK230 Kompressor package in the States, but now dropped to the options list for that grade.

The Value-Added Option Packages were duly revised to suit the new specifications: The 230 could be ordered with the K1 package (power seats and telescopic steering adjustment) for $850. Both cars were available with the $1545 K4 package, which added Xenon headlights, headlight washers and heated seats. The 'Sport Package' (SP1) was much the same, with AMG body panels, a 17-inch wheel and tyre setup, a silver-painted grille, 'Sport' badges and projector-beam foglights, although the cost went up to $4135. The only other package was the existing $1795 K2 one, featuring a mobile phone and CD-changer installation. There was a K2a variation listed now, though, adding voice control to the telephone operation for an extra $395. The regular options were carried over, with metallic paint at $625, heated seats at $620, and an automatic transmission – the latest 5AT coming with the 'Touchshift' facility, and commanding $950.

The Designo 'Electric Green Edition' was dropped for 2001 in favour of a 'Goldenrod' version, which was $4350 on the SLK230 Kompressor grade, and $300 more than that on the SLK320. The 'Copper' model continued, priced at $4800 and $5100 for the four- and six-cylinder cars, respectively.

The more powerful SLK320 was certainly welcomed in the press, with its artfully tuned exhaust (the result of several clinics) wooing even the hardest of journalists. Following the international press launch in the Canary Isles, *Motor Trend*'s Rik Paul noted: "The V6 finally fulfils the original promise of the SLK, blending quickness with refinement and a wonderful high-revving engine note. This can be coupled with a seamless six-speed manual transmission or a five-speed automatic with 'Touchshift'. Meanwhile, completing the package is a well-controlled suspension and responsive steering that provides good feedback and a precision feel.

"The SLK320 is still not a thoroughbred sports car; that's not its mission. This sophisticated roadster is a refined alternative to the raw adrenaline rush of, say, the more boisterous Boxster. It's a convertible when the weather's good, a securely sealed two-seater coupé when it's not, and an inviting choice for everyday driving, any day. Now with V6 power, the SLK also rates a couple notches higher on the fun scale, as well."

Car & Driver brought together a selection of German dropheads in the spring of 2000, including a manual SLK320 with

Above and overleaf: The SLK featured heavily in the 2001 Model Year range catalogue issued by Mercedes-Benz in the States.

MELBOURNE
SAO PAULO
BUENOS AIRES
IMOLA
MONTE CARLO
BARCELONA
MAGNY-COURS
MONTREAL
ZELTWEG
SILVERSTONE
BUDAPEST
HOCKENHEIM
SPA
MONZA
NÜRBURGRING
SUZUKA
MONTE CARLO 1937
MONZA 1938
LE MANS 1952
SPA 1955
JUAN FANGIO
LUIGI FAGIOLI
RUDOLF CARACCIOLA
STIRLING MOSS
After 107 years of speeding to victory, we think you'll enjoy what we've learned.
Every Mercedes is a highly capable performer. Because it inspires confidence and peace of mind. And also because it's just plain fun.
Almost all of our 2001 model lines offer an optional Sport Package that will take high performance—and high style—up a few notches.
AMG builds racecars for Mercedes. So it's easy to see why our AMG models for the street make car enthusiasts snap right to attention.
From the very first car race in 1894 to the most recent Formula One Driver Championship, we've done plenty of winning. And along the way, racing has taught us a lot about building street cars that perform. That endure. That can do things just a little better under the most challenging circumstances. So when you drive a Mercedes, you can share the thrill of our victories.
XUY 459
Sure, racing is instructive. But it's also lots of fun. And we know that if we build powerful, sure-handling and quick-stopping vehicles for the road, you're going to have just as much fun as we do. Exhilarating performance. Just part of The Mercedes Experience.
MIKA HAKKINEN
POLE POSITION
THE WINNERS
OUR TEAM
DAVID COULTHARD
WORLD CHAMPIONSHIP
VICTORY SHOWER
MELBOURNE 1999

The Models
It's like a candy store for grownups.

SLK Class
How hot is just right?

the AMG bodykit and rims, a BMW M Roadster, a 2.7-litre Porsche Boxster, and an Audi TT Quattro Roadster. The Benz recorded a 0-60 time of 6.8 seconds before breaking past the quarter-mile marker 8.3 seconds later, which was slower than all the others gathered, despite the Audi being heavier. Notwithstanding, the braking figures were good, as was the slalom result. The SLK was also significantly quieter and more frugal than its rivals. Its charm and balance of qualities earned it second place overall, with its "V6 power, V6 exhaust music, improved handling and high comfort quotient" scoring with the judges.

The extra support in the latest seats allowed the car's handling limits to be explored more readily. It was noted: "Although the steering still had some of the previous SLK's non-linear response, characterized by abrupt turn-in, the rest of its reflexes were honed to a far keener edge — improved roll stiffness, quicker transient responses — inspiring much higher confidence at the helm. Mercedes achieved this by a slight increase in spring rates, a 5mm (0.2in) reduction in ride height, an increase in the diameter of the front anti-roll bar, and the addition of a 16mm (0.6in) bar at the rear (the original had none). And let's not forget the new six-speed manual transmission, which replaces the clunky old five-speed. It's not as crisp as the Bimmer's gearbox, but it's the best yet in a Mercedes."

The spongy brake feel and irritating windblocker were pointed out as faults, and while more power would have been welcomed, the article summed things up by saying the SLK was "still more boulevardier than sports car, but tough to beat for comfort and four-seasons fun." Finishing on 94 points, the SLK was only two down on the Boxster and three ahead of the BMW and Audi – a good performance.

American advertising from early 2001. Note the extra lights still used on the front bumper inserts of US-spec cars.

Various views of the SLK320 for the UK market, including a look at the engine bay and interior – the latter sporting the optional leather trim and an automatic gearbox.

The rhd markets

The new car was already in the UK price lists by the first week of February 2000. Initially, the SLK200 Kompressor was priced at £26,390, with the SLK230 Kompressor at £29,550, and the SLK320 commanding £33,000. All three cars came with an automatic transmission (with cruise control), ESP, side airbags, and air-conditioning as standard, and the option of a six-speed manual gearbox. By the start of summer, while the sticker price remained unchanged, the entry-level model lost its air-conditioning, and a £640 price hike was applied to the other two grades.

Quirky British advertising for the face-lifted SLK.

Autocar tested a manual SLK320 with the optional 17-inch seven-spoke alloys (SA code 689) in August 2000, and having recorded a top speed of 149mph (238kph) and a 0-60 time of 7.0 seconds, loved the "wonderful engine and looks, slick six-speed gearbox, and folding roof." At the same time, the "limited luggage room and uncommunicative steering" were highlighted as points that were less appreciated.

Overall, though, the SLK320, which averaged an impressive 24.4mpg during its time with the magazine, was given a glowing report: "It's rare that an engine can single-handedly transform a car, but the SLK's new powerplant redefines the Mercedes' appeal, making it considerably more desirable than the supercharged model … The smooth and vocal V6 adds a deep layer of sophistication to an already desirable car."

The flexible engine was ably backed up by the 6MT: "The new manual gearbox makes the SLK even more of a pleasure to drive. It has a short, wrist-flick throw with none of the vagueness of traditional Mercedes 'boxes … Uniting the V6 and the excellent manual 'box has created a thoroughly engaging roadster." With further improved road manners, the magazine had no hesitation in giving the car four out of five stars.

By the end of the year, things had started to settle down on the model mix and pricing, with the SLK200 Kompressor listed at £24,490 with the automatic transmission becoming a £1450 option (air-conditioning added another £1270), the SLK230 Kompressor now £27,890 in manual guise (again, the 5AT unit was a £1450 extra), and the manual SLK320 £30,890, with an automatic gearbox adding £1450 to the invoice. Metallic paint

Interior and exterior views of the UK-spec SLK200 Kompressor model for the 2001 season. Note the manual gearbox and standard wheels on this car.

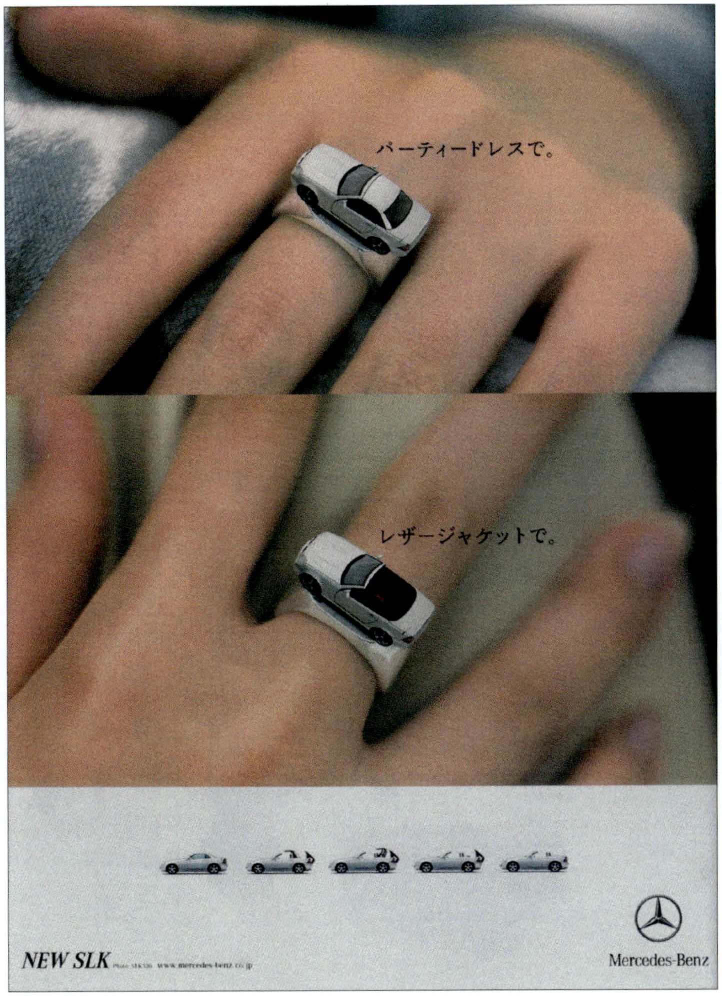

Two pieces of Japanese advertising from the early part of 2001. Note the US-style radio antenna, but the regular lighting used in Europe and the Antipodes.

was a £650 option, while leather trim set the owner back a further £1000. To put these prices into perspective, the basic contemporary BMW Z3 3.0i was £26,930, the Alfa 2.0TS Lusso Spider £26,193, and top Mazda MX-5 a reasonable £19,200.

In Japan, the line-up was restricted to the SLK230 Kompressor and SLK320 models, as in America. Both came with an automatic transmission, with the four-cylinder car priced at ¥4,950,000 (rhd only), and the V6 machine commanding ¥6,100,000, available in lhd or rhd guise.

Heading south, the new models were listed in Australia from the start of August, with the SLK200 Kompressor priced at $83,500 (or $86,600 with a 5AT), the SLK230 Kompressor at $93,600 (or $96,700 in automatic form), and the SLK320 at $112,500, which was sold in automatic guise only.

Smitten by the new V6 package for the SLK, which gave the car a 0-60 time of 8.1 seconds, *Wheels* magazine noted: "The V6 SLK's chassis is biased towards comfort, yet it remains impressive. The little Merc has a comfortable ride around town,

COLOUR & TRIM GUIDE

These are the coachwork and trim colours introduced on the face-lifted cars in February 2000. There were very few changes to the colour palette thereafter, so it's easier to chart them in one block. Please remember that the more exciting interior options are usually distinctive two-tone colour schemes.

Standard paintwork options

Black (040), Firn White, aka Glacier White (143), Magma Red (586), and Yellowstone, aka Sunburst Yellow (685). Firn White was replaced by Alabaster White (960) from June 2001.

Metallic paintwork options

Obsidian Black (197), Linarite Blue, aka Bahama Blue (352), Lazulite Blue, aka Sapphire Blue (372), Bernstein Red, aka Amber Red or Firemist Red (548), Brilliant Silver (744), and, from June 2000, Prismatine Green, aka Laguna Green (810). In August 2002, Prismatine Green was replaced by Andradite Green, aka Everest Green (816), and Cubanite Silver, aka Pewter Silver (723) was added as a new, additional colour.

Interior trim options

Anthracite (aka Charcoal) cloth (011) or leather (211/881), Merlin Blue cloth (012) or leather (212), Siam Beige (aka Sienna) leather (215), Magma Red (aka Crimson) cloth (017) or leather (217/887), and Lotus Yellow (aka Citrus) leather (219). From February 2002, Anthracite was the only cloth trim option remaining, and the Lotus Yellow leather shade had been superseded by an Alpaca Grey (888) one, although the latter was only available on the AMG car. The optional wood trim came with a choice of Bird's-Eye Maple or Calyptus Linea veneers.

especially on rough surfaces. Mind you, the SLK is no slouch on a challenging road, either. The chassis is well matched to the [Pirelli P6000] tyres, with firm but not harsh response. If there's a weak point, it's the steering, but only for the keenest of drivers. There's a woolliness just off centre that will annoy enthusiasts."

Australian prices crept up a touch on the manual fours during 2001, but the automatic models (including the six-cylinder SLK320) carried the same sticker price until September 2001.

The 2001 season in Germany

The Frankfurt Show, usually a showcase for German manufacturers, was a low-key affair for Mercedes in 2000, with the launch of the new C-Class Sports Coupé (C203) being the highlight. Not long after, the company withdrew from the US CART racing scene in order to concentrate its efforts on Formula One and touring cars – motorsport arenas in which the Mercedes-Benz marque was enjoying great success. Then, in January, visitors to the 2001 Detroit Show witnessed the official public launch of a couple of new C-Class models and the sporting SLK 32 AMG, the latter powered by a supercharged version of the V6 engine. Although the rapid two-seater wasn't available in America straight away, it went on sale in Europe during the same month as its Stateside debut.

As it happens, a new price list was required in Germany anyway, as the country was gearing up for the euro, and the exchange rate usefully hid a small increase of roughly two per cent on the basic SLK grades. As such, the SLK200 Kompressor was now valued at €26,900, with the SLK230 Kompressor €29,400, and the SLK320 €34,700. VAT was still 16 per cent in Germany, and this had to be added to these prices. This, and a corresponding increase in the cost of options, was about the only change applied to the existing line-up though, as all the standard specifications and the vast majority of optional extras were carried over from the April 2000 list. Two differences were noted; the old 794 AMG wheels were superseded by a new 767 design, which were similar but with narrower spokes, and the AMG sports seats (SA code 244) could be specified for €770 extra.

Before describing the SLK 32 AMG in detail, it's worth noting a few internal changes made to the original line-up. The transmission casing on the 6MT units used on the SLKs was modified in January 2001, along with the shift forks. The first and third gear cogs were changed a couple of times in the next few months, plus the first- and second-speed and third- and fourth-speed synchros that went with them. During the summer, the driveshaft and sixth-speed cogs were revised, along with the fifth- and sixth-speed synchronizer body and hydraulic control unit, leading to another change in the transmission casing. Other than a couple of modifications made to the third- and fourth-speed synchro in the tail-end of 2002 and 2003, the manual gearbox used in the face-lifted SLK range was otherwise unchanged until the end of production. All ratios, including the final-drive, were carried over, though, and it's doubtful whether anyone is even aware of the differences without tearing the 'box to bits.

Other changes included a new boot lock mechanism, introduced in November 2000, and a very minor revision to the rocker panel covers in May 2001; the lower air intake grille inserts on four-cylinder cars received attention at the same time.

The mighty supercharged V6 used in the SLK 32 AMG model.

The SLK 32 AMG

Priced at €49,000 (plus taxes) in Germany, the SLK 32 AMG model gave the compact two-seater Mercedes real sports car credentials. It was possible, by ordering option code 772 after June 2001 – when the AMG styling package was brought into line with the more aggressive-looking showroom model – to get something that looked similar, but the SLK 32 AMG was a fully-developed package that went far beyond a few styling tweaks.

The most important element in the SLK 32 AMG was the hand-built Type 112.960 engine – a supercharged version of

Continued on page 169

The new AMG car in standard trim, with its revised bodykit and double-spoke alloy wheels. Note also the purposeful-looking dual exhaust pipes.

Bernd Schneider, multiple German Touring Car (DTM) champion for Mercedes and AMG, enjoying himself in the SLK 32 AMG at the time of its launch.

AMG

AMG

The rather special interior of the SLK 32 AMG, with its unique black and grey leather trim on AMG sports seats, AMG steering wheel and instruments: thoughtful touches applied to the centre console, and its distinctive treadplates finishing off the package.

the 3199cc V6 found in the SLK320. Designated the M112 E32 ML AMG, as one would expect from AMG, there was much more to the unit than simply adding an IHI helical-type supercharger and an air-to-water intercooler. Indeed, it had a modified crankshaft, new con-rods and pistons, lighter camshafts operating on stiffer valve springs, a revised balance shaft, and an uprated oil pump. The exhaust system was all-new from the manifold back, too, with bigger mufflers after the catalytic converters, the addition of a collecting box before the back box, and dual stainless tailpipes poking out from under the rear valance.

With a Bosch ME management system and 9.0:1 compression ratio, it delivered 354bhp (over 60 per cent more power than the normally-aspirated V6) at 6100rpm, and a huge 332lbft of torque at 4400rpm. The fact that the car was 90kg (198lb) heavier than the SLK320 hardly seemed to matter with figures like that!

In an interview with *Road & Track*, Rolf Zimmermann, the drivetrain engineer, noted: "The main thing we wanted in this car was torque, lots of it. Of course, we looked at a number of ways to increase the power of the SLK, including putting in a bigger engine and turbocharging it. But we realized that the

Another early SLK 32 AMG, this one sporting the optional 767 alloys.

supercharger was the way to go, simply because of its packaging efficiency. It fits right between the two banks of cylinders."

In view of the torque output, there was no manual gearbox option. Instead, the engine was mated to an automatic transmission usually reserved for the larger V8s in the Mercedes-Benz range – the W5A580 (code 722.641), with cogs giving 3.59 on first, 2.19 on second, 1.41 on third, a direct fourth, and 0.83 on fifth; the final-drive ratio was set at 3.07:1. However, thanks to the 'Speedshift' feature, the shift programme was changed to give a more sporting, rapid response than that found on the silky smooth saloon applications, allowing enthusiasts to still drive with verve despite the lack of a third pedal. Upshifts were around 35 per cent faster, and torque converter lock-up from the lower gears helped enhance response still further. In addition, heavy braking prompted the gearbox to automatically drop a cog (or two) to ensure better pick-up once a hazard had been cleared, and the programme also took cornering attitudes into account, avoiding unwanted changes at a critical moment.

Although a governor kicked in at 156mph (250kph), official performance figures gave the SLK 32 AMG a 0-60 time of 5.2 seconds, which put it firmly in the supercar league. To cope with the additional speed, the AMG engineers revised the spring and damper settings, beefed up the front anti-roll bar, and increased the track a fraction. They left nothing to chance in the braking department either, specifying huge 334mm (13.1in) diameter vented discs at the front, and 300mm (11.8in) ones at the rear end. The chassis changes were rounded off with unique 17-inch AMG alloy wheels with five open spokes – one could call them a ten-spoke design as such. The 7.5J rims used up front sported 225/45 ZR-rated Pirelli P-Zero Rosso rubber, while the 8.5J wheels used at the rear came with 245/40 tyres.

Externally, the car came with the latest AMG bodykit offered on the regular cars, quickly identified by a more dramatic lower air intake arrangement, plus a discreet rear spoiler used on the SLK 32 AMG only, which helped reduce lift by around 50 per cent at the back. There were also special 'V6 Kompressor' badges added to the front wings. On opening a door, however, the various changes made to give the AMG car's interior a distinctive atmosphere became evident immediately, including the adoption of leather-trimmed AMG sports seats with eight-way power adjustment, integrated headrests and heaters (the latter meaning an uprated battery came as standard), an AMG leather-wrapped steering wheel (actually similar to the original SLK wheel but with heavier sections added to the rim above the upper spokes) with matching gearshift, darker-faced AMG instruments with a 300kph speedometer, black Bird's-Eye Maple wood trim, blackened controls for the standard air-conditioning, and AMG treadplates.

According to the colour charts, AMG cars came with the Bird's-Eye Maple veneer only – the other regular wood trim was not available, although Designo materials could be specified as an option. Leather trim was also standard (cloth was not available), with three trim choices, including all-black, black/red, and the new two-tone Anthracite/Alpaca Grey upholstery that was kept unique to the AMG machine.

Otherwise, options were virtually the same as those listed for the regular models, although a few of them were already made standard fitments on the AMG car, of course, and things like Designo trim came a fair bit cheaper. About the only area where choice was limited was in wheel selection, where one could order the 767 AMG wheels as an NCO, but was unable to specify any other rim without consulting the dealer.

In the States, where the car became available in the spring, the new AMG came third in a *Car & Driver* comparison test bringing together the supercharged Benz, a Chevrolet Corvette, BMW M Roadster and Porsche Boxster S. Not that any fault was implied: "The SLK 32 AMG was the champ at the drag strip, shooting through the quarter-mile in 13.0 seconds at 110mph (a tenth quicker than the Corvette and the BMW). By 140mph, the Merc had broken free of the pack, pulling 1.6 seconds ahead of the Chevy and 11.6 seconds in front of the Porsche. Want to lay rubber like an adolescent? Switch off ESP, brake-torque it a bit, and let 'er rip.

"But what impresses even more is the smoothness with which this V6 Kompressor gathers velocity. Stand on the gas, and the sport seat presses on the posterior instantly. That's your clue that an electric clutch has engaged the belt-driven IHI blower. With its Teflon-coated helical rotors twirling at 20,700rpm, it crams about 44lb of intercooled air per minute into the cylinders at twice atmospheric pressure. There's no perceptible lag or audible whistle, just big hairy hustle.

"The 'Sportshift' tranny is admittedly well-mated to the engine. Its torque converter locks up in every gear but first and reverse for efficiency, and the shifts are 35 per cent quicker than in lesser SLK slushboxes. It also downshifts under braking and does an admirable job of gear selection."

Having praised the chassis and braking, it came down to this: "[The SLK] won the test for one editor. The others grinned ever so slightly wider in the other two cars."

A little while later, *Motor Trend* put the AMG machine head-to-head against the BMW M Roadster, which was almost $10,000 cheaper than the Benz. The final verdict: "We thoroughly enjoyed these two breathtaking examples of BMW and Mercedes-Benz philosophy expertly honed to their sharpest points. Only much more expensive roadsters come close in terms of performance and panache. While the SLK 32 AMG earns points for its coupé-like folding hardtop, V8-like power, and elegant looks, the M Roadster's brilliant five-speed manual, bulldog demeanour, and comfortable cockpit more than gain them back." Fair comment.

The R230 SL was launched at the end of July 2001 – an altogether more sporting interpretation of the SL theme, in some ways harking back to the raw appeal of the original 'Gullwing' cars.

Actually, *Autocar* did a similar test in the UK, although it was well into the 2002 season before the AMG model was readily available in England. Anyway, the two offered breathtaking performance that was only possible to split with a very fine and accurate stopwatch. The BMW dismissed the 0-60 sprint in 4.8 seconds (0.1 less than the Mercedes), and the 157mph (251kph) top speed was one mile per hour faster, but basically they were neck-and-neck all the way. Interestingly, the BMW was far more frugal, averaging 20.1mpg (against 18.2 for the Stuttgart flyer), but after taking six different categories into consideration, it was the SLK that ultimately got the nod.

The speed was only part of the equation: "The performance is all the more astonishing for its linearity. Past conversions concerning torque plateaus need to be reassessed now that we've driven this thing. At 2300rpm, the SLK nonchalantly offers up 89 per cent of that massive twisting force, which makes overtaking an utter joy … And it's got character. The supercharger tends to cover most of the intake and V6 noises under the bonnet, but fix an ear on its backside and those tailpipes make a terrific noise."

Summing up: "As a package – huge torque, a brilliant automatic gearbox and that [power top] – it gels in a way the BMW cannot match. The SLK 32 AMG is a reminder that raw muscle can be a satisfying substitute for pure ability."

The 2002 season

The all-new R230 SL was announced at the end of July 2001 in readiness for the 2002 Model Year. By adopting the vario-roof design that had made its debut on the R170 SLK, this was the first SL to move away from a traditional soft top (with separate hardtop) configuration. An R230 version of the SL 55 AMG was launched at the 2001 Frankfurt Show, along with a couple of other AMGs, with the supercharged engine duly winning several awards.

Cover and selected pages from the domestic catalogue printed in August 2001. Later, the title changed to 'Die Roadster Der SLK-Klasse,' although the contents were the same.

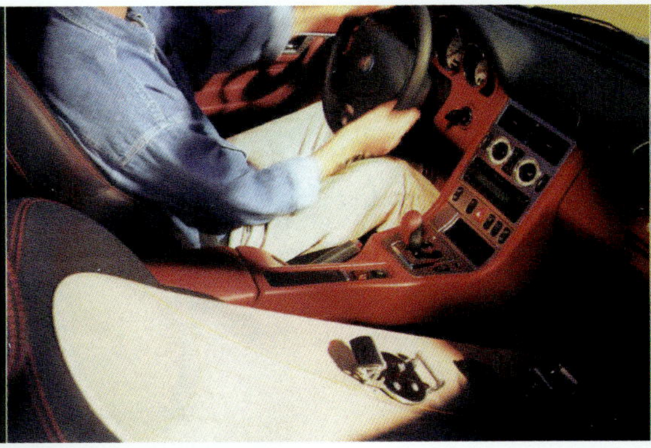

1.

2.

3.

1. Neue Stoßfänger. Hier zu sehen für die 4-Zylinder-Motoren.
2. Die Außenspiegel mit integrierten Zusatzblinkleuchten.
3. Blinker und Bremslichter sind in die dreieckigen Rückleuchten integriert.
4. Serie im SLK 200 KOMPRESSOR: das Leichtmetallrad im 7-Loch-Design.
5. Serie im SLK 230 KOMPRESSOR: das 16"-Leichtmetallrad im 6-Speichen-Design.
6. Serie im SLK 320: das 16"-Leichtmetallrad im 5-Speichen-Design.

4.

5.

6.

29

The page showing the standard wheel designs for the non-AMG cars is particularly useful.

For the 2002 season, the normally-aspirated V6 engine was given a number of upgrades, including revised exhaust manifolds, a new air filter assembly and mass airflow sensor, block preheater, starter motor, alternator, PAS pump and air-conditioning pump. Naturally, these changes found their way onto the SLK320 in due course, as did the other mods made to the oil cooler, timing chain cover, water pump and crankshaft.

In America, the SLK230 Kompressor continued for 2002 at $500 more than before, and the SLK320 continued at $900 more. These were joined by the AMG version, added to the line-up at $54,900, with its supercharged V6 and 'Sportshift' 5AT, AMG exhaust system, 17-inch double-spoke alloys, bodykit (including a colour-keyed rear spoiler), and the AMG interior touches found on European models.

British advertising for the 2002 season.

Two new Designo models were added for 2002, replacing the old versions. Both were priced at $4800 for the supercharged four, or $5100 for the SLK320. The 'Silver Edition' featured silver metallic paint, a charcoal interior with silver Nappa leather and charcoal cinnamora trim, charcoal floormats with silver leather piping, and silver leather on the bars behind the seats; heated front seats were required. The other was the 'Terra Cotta Edition' with mocha black metallic paint, a charcoal interior with terra cotta Nappa leather and natural cinnamora trim, charcoal floormats with terra cotta leather piping, and terra cotta leather on the roll-over hoops. Again, heated front seats were required, either via a single option or the K4 package.

Regular options were carried over, as were the Value-Added Option Packages, although the 'Sport Package' was obviously not available on the SLK 32 AMG model, and the K4 option was cheaper on that car, too, as heated seats were already standard on the AMG grade.

In Britain, the 2002 Model Year SLK200 Kompressor model commanded £24,790, the SLK230 Kompressor, £28,240, and the SLK320, £31,240. An automatic transmission added £1450 to the invoice on all cars, until the SLK 32 AMG arrived in February 2002, that is, for the £44,290 supercharged machine came with a 5AT only.

The Japanese line-up was much the same, but oddly, for 2002, the SLK320 was dropped from Australian showrooms, leaving only the SLK200 Kompressor at $86,600 and SLK230 Kompressor at $95,400 to hold the fort for a little while, with an automatic gearbox costing an extra $1300 on both grades. However, the AMG model – which according to *Wheels* was "fantastic, rain, hail or shine" – went on sale at the start of the season, ably filling the gap. Introduced at $154,500, not long after the pricing on the fours was adjusted, with the automatic 2-litre car and manual 2.3-litre machine becoming a little cheaper. The CLK came on line at this time, by the way, ranging in price from $86,900 all the way up to $193,900 for the CLK 55 AMG.

Meanwhile, at the end of 2001, with annual car production reaching almost one-and-a-quarter million units, a small ceremony was held at the Sindelfingen plant to commemorate the production of 20,000,000 passenger cars at the plant since the cessation of hostilities in WWII. As the year drew to a close, the four-cylinder SLKs gained a new thermostat and covering for

The attractive SLK 'Special Edition' model, launched in the spring of 2002.

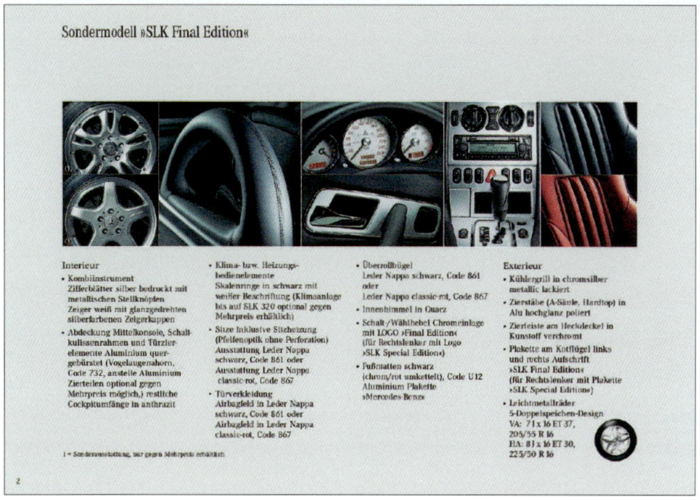

Sondermodell »SLK Final Edition«

Interieur
- Kombiinstrument
  Zifferblätter silber bedruckt mit metallischen Stellknöpfen
  Zeiger weiß mit glanzgedrehten silberfarbenen Zeigerkappen
- Abdeckung Mittelkonsole, Schaltkulissenrahmen und Türzierelemente Aluminium quergebürstet (Vogelaugenahorn, Code 732, anstelle Aluminium Zierteilen optional gegen Mehrpreis möglich,) restliche Cockpitumfänge in anthrazit
- Klima- bzw. Heizungsbedienelemente
  Skalenringe in schwarz mit weißer Beschriftung (Klimaanlage bis auf SLK 320 optional gegen Mehrpreis erhältlich)
- Sitze inklusive Sitzheizung (Pfeifenoptik ohne Perforation)
  Ausstattung Leder Nappa schwarz, Code 861 oder
  Ausstattung Leder Nappa classic-rot, Code 867
- Türverkleidung
  Airbagfeld in Leder Nappa schwarz, Code 861 oder
  Airbagfeld in Leder Nappa classic-rot, Code 867
- Überrollbügel
  Leder Nappa schwarz, Code 861 oder
  Leder Nappa classic-rot, Code 867
- Innenhimmel in Quarz
- Schalt-/Wählhebel Chromeinlage mit LOGO »Final Edition«
  (für Rechtslenker mit Logo »SLK Special Edition«)
- Fußmatten schwarz (chrom/rot umkettelt), Code U12
  Aluminium Plakette »Mercedes-Benz«

Exterieur
- Kühlergrill in chromsilber metallic lackiert
- Zierstäbe (A-Säule, Hardtop) in Alu hochglanz poliert
- Zierleiste am Heckdeckel in Kunstoff verchromt
- Plakette am Kotflügel links und rechts Aufschrift »SLK Final Edition«
  (für Rechtslenker mit Plakette »SLK Special Edition«)
- Leichtmetallräder
  5-Doppelspeichen-Design
  VA: 7 J x 16 ET 37, 205/55 R 16
  HA: 8 J x 16 ET 30, 225/50 R 16

1 = Sonderausstattung, nur gegen Mehrpreis erhältlich

2

German paperwork relating to the SLK 'Final Edition' of 2003 vintage.

the front of the rocker cover, but there were no other changes of note during this period, other than a new black box for the 5AT unit, and a modified rear axle assembly and driveshafts for all SLKs.

Not long after, in January 2002, the new W211 E-Class made its debut at the Brussels Show. As it happens, the cost of SLK motoring increased in Germany in the same month, with the SLK200 Kompressor going up to €27,350, the SLK230 Kompressor up to €29,850, and the SLK320 now commanding €35,150. The AMG model was €450 more expensive than at the time of its debut, now listed at €49,450. Standard specifications remained unchanged, however, as did the scope of the option list. One or two option prices were revised, including those of the alloy wheels (up €5 across the board), seat heaters (also €5 more), the AMG seats and bodykit, uprated battery, headlight washers and self-dimming mirrors (all up by €10), and the automatic gearbox (up €40). Leather trim and metallic and Designo paintwork also increased in price, but only by €5 in most cases, and the cost of the radio/cassette units went up by €10. One can see that the hike was hardly like the British Leyland ones of the 1970s, which, on top of being issued every few months, were generally pegged two or three times above the inflation rate!

A couple of weeks later, the company announced the new M271 four-cylinder engine incorporating a number of advanced technologies pointing the way towards the future, with supercharging, intercooling, four valves per cylinder, adjustable camshaft positioning, and Lanchester-type balance shafts being part of the specification. One of the first applications was the C209-type CLK, launched at the Geneva Show; a drophead version followed a year later.

At the end of April 2002, the company launched the SLK 'Special Edition' model, which was available based on the two four-cylinder cars and the SLK320. The price was only €1700 over and above the regular SLK200 Kompressor, and as little as €1300 more than the basic V6 car. For the little extra, the buyer received attractive 7.5J x 17 seven-spoke wheels shod with 225/45 rubber, and a number of interior enhancements. While the aluminium-style trim was normal, the black Nappa leather trim certainly wasn't; nor were the seat heaters, contrasting headlining, special gearshift, silver-coloured dials with white pointers, blacked out HVAC controls, and unique footmats with silver piping. Naturally, to finish the package, small silver and black badges were added to the front wings to give the car – which was sold all over Europe – a little extra kudos.

The 2003 model year

A change was made to the automatic transmission (including the torque converter) on the SLK 32 AMG model at this time, just as the 2003 season was starting, along with a new clutch plate for the SLK320. But it was the exhibits at the 2002 Paris Salon that grabbed the headlines, with face-lifted versions of the W220 S-Class and C215 CL models on display, as well as new C- and E-Class variants, and a fresh six-cylinder R230 SL model – the SL350.

Dr Thomas Weber took over responsibility for R&D on the first day of 2003, while the 2003 Detroit Show, which opened on 11 January, witnessed the launch of the twelve-cylinder SL600 model, as well as that of the E-Class estate.

Not long after, in February 2003, the price of SLK motoring went up again, with €450 added to the basic cost of the four-cylinder cars and the SLK320, while the SLK 32 AMG was given a €650 price hike, taking it to just over €50,000 before tax.

As before, not all options increased in price in line with the base car, although quite a few did. The Designo paint, all-weather tyres, anti-dazzle mirrors, steering column adjustment and cassette/CD holders all went up €5, leather trim, the uprated battery, heated windscreen washers, luggage rack and telephone antenna were up €10 apiece, metallic paint cost €15 more than before, and the alloy wheel options, automatic transmission, Designo leather, garage door opener and Audio 10 stereo with a CD player, each went up by €20.

These were to be the last price increases applied to the R170 SLK, although the last week of February 2003 also witnessed the announcement of another special SLK model – the SLK 'Final Edition'. Based on the same grades as the 'Special Edition' had been, the SLK200 Kompressor version was listed at €29,400, the one based on the SLK230 Kompressor came in at €2300 more, and the SLK320-based model, €36,900. The extra money secured special 16-inch five-spoke alloys (with double-spokes, like the SLK 32 AMG wheels), a silver finish on the radiator grille, polished aluminium trim pieces on the A-posts, a chrome

Nicky Barrett, National Dressage Champion, pictured with her mount and her SLK320 from Mercedes-Benz UK.

boot plinth, and commemorative badges on the front wings. Inside, the 'Final Edition' came with brushed aluminium trim pieces rather than engine-turned ones, light silver gauge faces, silver clock and odometer buttons, a special gearshift, blacked-out HVAC controls, seat heaters, red or black Nappa leather trim (including matching roll-over hoops, door inserts and the unique ribbed seat inserts), contrasting headlining, and special floormats. One could specify two other wheel designs and Bird's-Eye Maple trim at extra cost, but the basic package was already quite spectacular.

As far as the SLK was concerned, the line-up and prices were basically carried over for 2003 in the States, even down to the Designo models and options. On saying that, the cost of metallic paint became a bit more complicated, although prices still started at $640 nonetheless.

In the UK, the non-AMG cars started the 2003 season about £290 more expensive than before, with the SLK 32 AMG receiving a minor £170 price hike. By the spring of 2003, however, another increase had been applied, taking the SLK200 Kompressor to £25,455, the SLK230 Kompressor to £28,955, and the SLK320 to £31,955. An automatic transmission was a £1450 option on these cars, but standard on the SLK 32 AMG, which by now cost £45,125.

Even though the R171 was waiting in the wings, the crankcase and front section of the cylinder head cover were changed on the four-cylinder cars at the end of June 2003.

For 2003, Japanese buyers could choose from the SLK230 Kompressor model at ¥4,800,000, the SLK320 at ¥900,000 more in standard form, or ¥6,300,000 in 'Sportline' guise, and the SLK 32 AMG, which commanded ¥7,700,000. This advert also shows the C-Class Sports Coupé.

The German engineers were nothing if not thorough! Indeed, they were still making modifications to the roof assembly, and new rear axle drive flanges were introduced on the two fours and the SLK320 model as late as December 2003.

End of the line

September 2003 saw the announcement of the 7G-Tronic automatic gearbox, a 7AT unit developed in-house to give better performance, and improved economy at the same time. It was first seen on the eight-cylinder cars, including the SL range. Hardly pausing for breath, Mercedes displayed the SLR McLaren, Vision CLS study vehicle (eventually launched as the supremely elegant CLS production car in March 2004), a four-door Smart model, and a bi-fuel version of the E-Class at the 2003 Frankfurt Show. The bi-fuel car was a sign of the times, although the Stuttgart maker was, in fact, experimenting with all sorts of 'green' technology behind the scenes, ranging from fuel cell vehicles to conventional EVs, and diesel-based hybrids.

THE CHRYSLER CROSSFIRE

The Chrysler Crossfire was an interesting spin-off from the Daimler-Benz and Chrysler merger, built by Karmann in Germany between February 2003 and December 2007. Why is it included in this book? Well, the platform and many of the components are shared with those of the R170 SLK320, with the rare SRT-6 variants coming with the supercharged AMG engine. The first season was restricted to coupé bodies, although a convertible augmented the line for the 2005 season onwards. In all, 76,014 cars were produced during the Crossfire's life cycle, with just under 43,000 of them having the closed bodywork. The SRT-6, available with both body configurations, was indeed rare, with just 4071 sold in total, which included 2571 coupés.

The 3.2-litre Chrysler Crossfire coupé attracting press attention at the 2003 Tokyo Show.

Just before Christmas 2003, a new 3.5-litre V6 (M272) engine was presented to the press. Using four-valve-per-cylinder technology, it was first seen in the new R171 SLK, launched at the 2004 Geneva Show. At the same time, the company introduced a new clear coat paint using advanced nanotechnology to help

The SLR McLaren, seen here at the 2003 Tokyo Show.

An SLK on display at the 2004 San Jose Show, a couple of months before the R171 series was introduced.

prevent coachwork scratches. The E, S, CL, SL and SLK ranges were the first to employ this new paint, although it spread to the other model lines soon after.

In the meantime, the American SLK line-up had the same basic models listed for 2004, and only a fraction more expensive – the SLK230 Kompressor had a $39,600 sticker price, the SLK320 came in at $45,050, and the AMG car commanded $55,450. As *Motor Trend* noted: "Once labelled a 'girl's car' with a just-adequate four-cylinder engine and just-only automatic transmission, the SLK line has matured nicely after the addition of a vigorous 215bhp (SAE) V6 model, the haulin' 349bhp SLK 32 AMG and, for the lesser two SLKs, a standard six-speed manual."

Options were realigned slightly, with automatic transmission now costing $60 more, the SP1 package being renamed the 'AMG Sport Package,' the old K1 one now being called the 'Comfort Package,' the K4 one becoming the 'Lighting Package,' and the former K2 package being split, allowing buyers to go for the CD-changer or mobile phone as separate items; the CD unit was $410, with phones costing $1595 upwards.

The complete Designo cars were carried over, albeit $100 more expensive than before, but new for the SLK230 Kompressor and SLK320 models was the $1600 SLK 'Special Edition Package,' which included special sport seats with ribbed inserts and the roll-over bars trimmed in charcoal Nappa leather, unique 17-inch wheels, a rear spoiler (as per the AMG model), a silver-painted radiator grille, high-gloss A-posts, special badges on the front wings, a 'Special Edition' chrome gearknob, CD-changer, Calyptus wood trim (brushed aluminium could be specified on white cars if the owner wished), and silver-coloured instrument faces. Possible colours included the solid black, white and red shades, along with Pewter Metallic and Brilliant Silver Metallic. On the subject of colours, the Sapphire Blue Metallic, Laguna Green Metallic and Sunburst Yellow hues were dropped from the US range at this time, along with the blue and yellow leather trim options.

The US price list issued in February 2004 was exactly the same as the July 2003 one, except the two Designo packages both had another $100 added to them. Just for the record, and to put things into perspective, the R171 was introduced at $46,250 in SLK350 guise, and $60,500 in SLK 55 AMG form.

For 2004, prices went up by an average of £400 across the UK SLK line. The last listing, issued in June 2004, pegged the SLK200 Kompressor at £25,760, the SLK230 Kompressor at £29,300, the SLK320 at £32,370, and the SLK 32 AMG at £45,640. The new R171 cars were duly listed from the first week of July 2004.

In Japan, the last of the SLK230 Kompressor models carried a ¥5,040,000 sticker price, with the 'Special Edition' version being ¥157,500 more. The SLK320 commanded ¥5,985,000, although

The 2004 MY 'Special Edition Package' as sold in the States. This Magma Red car was featured in an advertising spread in *Architectural Digest* magazine.

The two Designo cars sold in the US during the 2004 season.

An SLK320, seen here with the Sport Package.

The arrival of the R171 SLK signalled the end of the R170's run. The outgoing car had been incredibly successful, though, with well over 300,000 units sold.

the SLK350 that replaced it in the early autumn was introduced at ¥6,720,000, making it a fair bit more pricey than its predecessor. The AMG car bowed out at ¥8,085,000.

In Australia, during the spring of 2004, the SLK line-up was still an extensive one, with the SLK200 Kompressor at $86,175 in automatic guise, the SLK230 Kompressor at $96,275, the SLK320 at $112,075, and the SLK 32 AMG at $154,075. At this time, while the CLK range started at $90,000, the SL was close to $300,000 for the base model! As for outside competitors, the Mazda MX-5 was less than half price of the cheapest SLK (about $41,000), with the Toyota MR2 Spyder tagged at $49,230, and the Porsche Boxster ranging from $108,500 to $140,100. The new car eventually made it into Australian showrooms during the tail-end of summer, introduced at a competitive $109,400 in manual form, or $112,900 with the seven-speed automatic.

With the debut of the R171, the fate of the SLK was sealed – the last of the R170 breed rolling out in April 2004. Regarding the 140,503 later, face-lifted cars, of the 55,449 SLK200 Kompressors built, 21,878 were equipped with an automatic transmission, and no less than 36,987 of the 47,305 SLK230 Kompressor models built had the 5AT unit. As for the SLK320, no less than 28,854 of the 33,416 produced were fitted with an automatic transmission, while the ultra-rare SLK 32 AMG accounted for another 4333 SLK sales, all of which having an automatic gearbox. When added together with the original SLK run, total R170 sales amounted to no less than 311,222 units.

Tailpiece.

Appendix I

Year-by-year range details

This appendix brings together the brief specifications for all R170-series models, arranged in chronological/engine size order. The first column shows the vehicle type, the second column shows the basic engine details (to be used in conjunction with Appendix II), whilst the third contains any useful notes, including the main market (if nothing is listed, one can assume worldwide sales, while the cars with 'European market' against them are not always restricted to EU countries – please refer to the main text for definitive details). Only production road cars are listed for each model year (MY).

1997

SLK200 (170.435)	M111.946	Pilot build from October 1995. Full-scale production starts July 1996. European market.
SLK200 Kompressor (170.445)	M111.943	Pilot build from November 1995. Full-scale production starts August 1996. European market.
SLK230 Kompressor (170.447)	M111.973	Pilot build from October 1995. Full-scale production starts July 1996.

1998

SLK200 (170.435)	M111.946	European market.
SLK200 Kompressor (170.445)	M111.943	European market.
SLK230 Kompressor (170.447)	M111.973	US sales started January 1997, but the car was classed as an early 1998 model.

1999

SLK200 (170.435)	M111.946	European market.
SLK200 Kompressor (170.445)	M111.943	European market.
SLK230 Kompressor (170.447)	M111.973	

2000		
SLK200 (170.435)	M111.946	European market. To February 2000.
SLK200 Kompressor (170.445)	M111.943	European market. To February 2000.
SLK230 Kompressor (170.447)	M111.973	To February 2000.
SLK200 Kompressor (170.444)	M111.958	Face-lift model. Pilot build from July 1999. Full-scale production starts February 2000. European market.
SLK230 Kompressor (170.449)	M111.983	Face-lift model. Pilot build from June 1999. Full-scale production starts February 2000.
SLK320 (170.465)	M112.947	Pilot build from June 1999. Full-scale production starts February 2000.
2001		
SLK200 Kompressor (170.444)	M111.958	European market.
SLK230 Kompressor (170.449)	M111.983	
SLK320 (170.465)	M112.947	
SLK 32 AMG (170.466)	M112.960	Pilot build from August 2000. Full-scale production starts January 2001.
2002		
SLK200 Kompressor (170.444)	M111.958	European market.
SLK230 Kompressor (170.449)	M111.983	
SLK320 (170.465)	M112.947	
SLK 32 AMG (170.466)	M112.960	
2003		
SLK200 Kompressor (170.444)	M111.958	European market.
SLK230 Kompressor (170.449)	M111.983	
SLK320 (170.465)	M112.947	
SLK 32 AMG (170.466)	M112.960	
2004		
SLK200 Kompressor (170.444)	M111.958	European market. To April 2004.
SLK230 Kompressor (170.449)	M111.983	To April 2004.
SLK320 (170.465)	M112.947	To April 2004.
SLK 32 AMG (170.466)	M112.960	To March 2004.

Appendix II

Engine specifications

The following is a survey of all the mainstream production engines employed in the R170-series models featured in this book, complete with the leading specifications and any other notes of interest. One should bear in mind that engines with 'Europe' listed as the main market are not always restricted to EU countries, and are occasionally restricted to certain areas – please refer to the main text for definitive details.

Type 111.943 (M111 E20 ML)

Production (MY)	1997-2000
Cylinders	Straight-four, water-cooled
Main bearings	Five, in cast iron block
Valve operation	Dohc, 16v, in alloy head
Bore & stroke	89.9 x 78.7mm
Cubic capacity	1998cc
Compression ratio	8.5:1
Fuel delivery system	Fuel-injection, plus supercharger
Engine management	Bosch ME
Power @ rpm	192bhp (141kW) DIN @ 5300
Torque @ rpm	199lbft (270Nm) DIN @ 2500-4800
Main market	Europe

Notes: Used in the SLK200 Kompressor model from August 1996 to February 2000.

Type 111.946 (M111 E20)

Production (MY)	1997-2000
Cylinders	Straight-four, water-cooled
Main bearings	Five, in cast iron block
Valve operation	Dohc, 16v, in alloy head
Bore & stroke	89.9 x 78.7mm
Cubic capacity	1998cc
Compression ratio	10.4:1
Fuel delivery system	Fuel-injection
Engine management	VDO MSE
Power @ rpm	136bhp (100kW) DIN @ 5500
Torque @ rpm	140lbft (190Nm) DIN @ 3700-4500
Main market	Europe

Notes: Used in the SLK200 from July 1996 to February 2000.

Type 111.958 (M111 E20 EVO ML)

Production (MY)	2000-2004
Cylinders	Straight-four, water-cooled
Main bearings	Five, in cast iron block
Valve operation	Dohc, 16v, in alloy head
Bore & stroke	89.9 x 78.7mm
Cubic capacity	1998cc
Compression ratio	9.5:1
Fuel delivery system	Fuel-injection, plus supercharger
Engine management	Siemens SIM 4 LE

Power @ rpm	163bhp (120kW) DIN @ 5300
Torque @ rpm	170lbft (230Nm) DIN @ 2500-4800
Main market	Europe

Notes: Used in the SLK200 Kompressor model from February 2000 to April 2004.

Type 111.973 (M111 E23 ML)

Production (MY)	1997-2000
Cylinders	Straight-four, water-cooled
Main bearings	Five, in cast iron block
Valve operation	Dohc, 16v, in alloy head
Bore & stroke	90.9 x 88.4mm
Cubic capacity	2295cc
Compression ratio	8.8:1
Fuel delivery system	Fuel-injection, plus supercharger
Engine management	Bosch ME
Power @ rpm	193bhp (142kW) DIN @ 5300
Torque @ rpm	207lbft (280Nm) DIN @ 2500-4800
Main market	Worldwide

Notes: Used in the SLK230 Kompressor from July 1996 to February 2000.

Type 111.983 (M111 E23 EVO ML)

Production (MY)	2000-2004
Cylinders	Straight-four, water-cooled
Main bearings	Five, in cast iron block
Valve operation	Dohc, 16v, in alloy head
Bore & stroke	90.9 x 88.4mm
Cubic capacity	2295cc
Compression ratio	9.0:1
Fuel delivery system	Fuel-injection, plus supercharger
Engine management	Siemens SIM 4 LE
Power @ rpm	197bhp (145kW) DIN @ 5500
Torque @ rpm	207lbft (280Nm) DIN @ 2500-5000
Main market	Worldwide

Notes: Used in the SLK230 Kompressor from February 2000 to April 2004.

The M112 V6 engine in an SLK320 from 2000.

Type 112.947 (M112 E32)

Production (MY)	2000-2004
Cylinders	90-degree V6, water-cooled
Main bearings	Four, in alloy block
Valve operation	Sohc per bank, 18v, in alloy head
Bore & stroke	89.9 x 84.0mm
Cubic capacity	3199cc
Compression ratio	10.0:1
Fuel delivery system	Fuel-injection
Engine management	Bosch ME
Power @ rpm	218bhp (160kW) DIN @ 5700
Torque @ rpm	229lbft (310Nm) DIN @ 3000-4600
Main market	Worldwide

Notes: Used in the SLK320 model from February 2000 to April 2004.

Type 112.960 (M112 E32 ML AMG)

Production (MY)	2001-2004
Cylinders	90-degree V6, water-cooled
Main bearings	Four, in alloy block
Valve operation	Sohc per bank, 18v, in alloy head
Bore & stroke	89.9 x 84.0mm
Cubic capacity	3199cc
Compression ratio	9.0:1
Fuel delivery system	Fuel-injection, plus supercharger
Engine management	Bosch ME
Power @ rpm	354bhp (260kW) DIN @ 6100
Torque @ rpm	332lbft (450Nm) DIN @ 4400
Main market	Worldwide

Notes: Used in the SLK 32 AMG model from January 2001 to March 2004.

Appendix III

Chassis numbers & production figures

Chassis numbers

The body codes and chassis start numbers for each model type:

Type	Model Year	Body Code	Chassis No
SLK200	1997-2000	R170.E20	WDB170435**
SLK200 Komp.	2000-2004	R170.E20	WDB170444**
SLK200 Komp.	1997-2000	R170.E20	WDB170445**
SLK230 Komp.	1997-2000	R170.E23	WDB170447**
SLK230 Komp.	2000-2004	R170.E23	WDB170449**
SLK320	2000-2004	R170.E32	WDB170465**
SLK 32 AMG	2001-2004	R170.E32	WDB170466**

Note: The first asterisk in the above chassis numbers is to be replaced by a '1' for left-hand drive, or a '2' for right-hand drive. The second asterisk is to be replaced by a letter ('F' through 'H') to show the car was built in the Bremen plant, followed by a sequential six-digit production serial number, starting on 000001. The SLK200 Kompressor entry for 2000-2004 looks odd, but it is correct.

For America and certain other countries, the 17-digit VIN number starts with 'WDB' to identify Daimler-Benz as the maker. The next four digits describe the model (with 'K' for 170-series, followed by 'K' for a drophead body, then a model key, such as '49' which is a shortened version of 170.449). The eighth digit shows restraint systems, and the ninth is simply a check digit, which is a number ('0' to '9') or an 'X' in place of the number ten. The tenth gives the year of manufacture, which is defined by letters and numbers (S = 1995, T = 1996, V = 1997, W = 1998, X = 1999, Y = 2000, 1 = 2001, 2 = 2002, 3 = 2003, and 4 = 2004). Next is a letter for the Bremen plant ('F' through 'H'), followed by a six-digit sequential serial number.

Build numbers

Production quantities for each model type, arranged by engine size and basic type:

Type	Model Year	Number built
SLK200	1997-2000	44,846
SLK200 Komp.	1997-2000	12,353
SLK230 Komp.	1997-2000	113,520
SLK200 Komp.	2000-2004	55,449
SLK230 Komp.	2000-2004	47,305
SLK320	2000-2004	33,416
SLK 32 AMG	2001-2004	4333

A different breakdown of the build numbers, this time showing how many of each model type was produced within a given calendar year (CY), including the pre-production prototypes. Unfortunately, the early normally-aspirated SLK200 and the supercharged version of the 2-litre model were batched together in the original annual data provided to the German government, hence the lack of a more accurate number for each type:

Year	SLK200 & SLK200K	Early SLK230K
1995 CY	13	18
1996 CY	3156	5023
1997 CY	15,755	32,390
1998 CY	17,794	37,028
1999 CY	19,356	36,789
2000 CY	1125	2272

Year	Late SLK200K	Late SLK230K	SLK320 V6	SLK 32 AMG
1999 CY	26	77	67	–
2000 CY	15,898	15,860	14,002	10
2001 CY	16,550	13,152	10,287	2193
2002 CY	11,581	9987	5340	1336
2003 CY	9811	7260	3377	742
2004 CY	1583	969	343	52

Overall production figures

A table showing a summary of the annual production (by CY) for all R170 SLK models combined (including prototypes), followed by a cumulative figure, valid at the end of each calendar year:

Year	Number built	Cumulative production
1995 CY	31	31
1996 CY	8179	8210
1997 CY	48,145	56,355
1998 CY	54,822	111,177
1999 CY	56,315	167,492
2000 CY	49,167	216,659
2001 CY	42,182	258,841
2002 CY	28,244	287,085
2003 CY	21,190	308,275
2004 CY	2947	311,222
Total R170-series models built		**311,222**

Also from Veloce Publishing ...

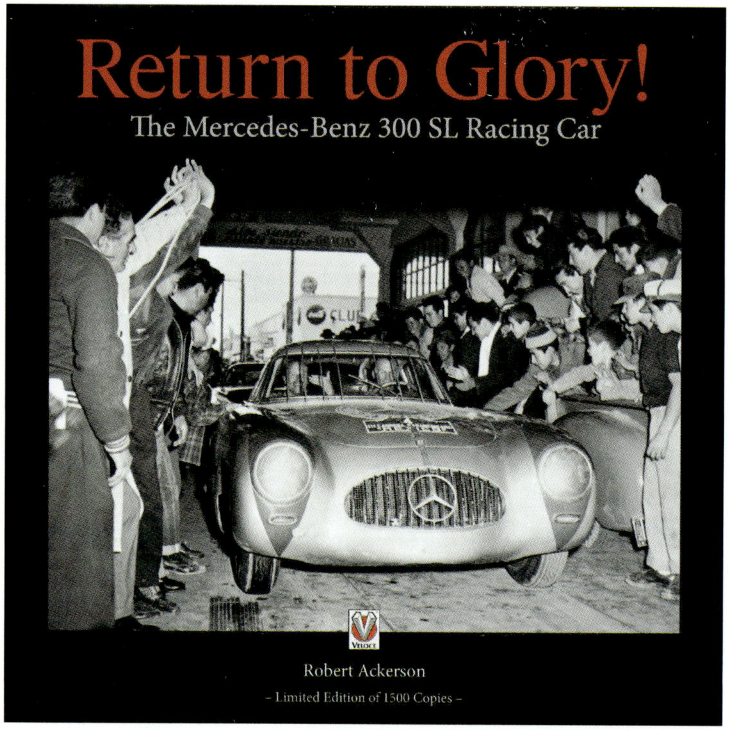

Return to Glory!

The Mercedes-Benz 300 SL Racing Car

Robert Ackerson

The 300 SL's 1952 debut was the culmination of a long, difficult road back to racing for Mercedes-Benz after a 13 year break. This book vividly depicts the 300 SL's performance in the five races in which it competed in that year, and tells the story of how it became the most successful competition sports car that season. Through dramatic photographs and stirring text, one of the greatest years of sports car racing is brought to life, filled with automobiles prepared by great factory teams, driven by men who were national sporting idols, and raced under gruelling conditions unique to the age.

ISBN: 978-1-845846-17-6
Hardback • 25x25cm • 44 pages • 126 pictures
£75 UK/$120 USA (Prices subject to change. P&P extra)

Racing for Mercedes-Benz

A Dictionary of the 240 Fastest Drivers of the Marque

Hartmut Lehbrink

Of the vast number of drivers who have competed for Mercedes-Benz and its ancestors in the past 115 years, famous and obscure, the 240 fastest are examined in this volume. A unique insight into some of the quickest drivers the world has ever seen.

ISBN: 978-1-845840-44-0
Hardback • 27x21.5cm • 256 pages • 350 pictures
£35 UK/$69.95 USA (Prices subject to change. P&P extra)

For more information on our titles, visit our websites, email info@veloce.co.uk or call +44(0)1305 260068

www.veloce.co.uk • www.velocebooks.com • digital.veloce.co.uk

Index

Mercedes-Benz, as well as Daimler-Benz, DaimlerChrysler and Daimler AG, along with their subsidiaries and products, are mentioned throughout the book.